Country Railways

Country Railways

Text by Paul Atterbury

Photographs by Ian Burgum

WEIDENFELD & NICOLSON, LONDON

Text © Paul Atterbury 1996
Photographs © Burgum Boorman Ltd 1996

Paul Atterbury has asserted his right to be identified as the Author of this work.

First published in Great Britain in 1996 by
George Weidenfeld & Nicolson Ltd
The Orion Publishing Group
Orion House
5, Upper St Martin's Lane
London WC2H 9EA

A CIP catalogue record for this book is available from the British Library.

House editor: Richard Atkinson
Text editor: Jonathan Hilton
Designer: Martin Richards
Printed and bound in Italy

Contents

Introduction

St Erth to St Ives

One of the best of Britain's seaside railways is the short branch from St Erth to St Ives, its route being a succession of delightful views of the Cornish coast. In evening light, the train nears Carbis Bay, high above Porth Kidney Sands.

The Duke of Wellington and William Wordsworth probably had only one thing in common – their mutual dislike of railways. The Duke considered the train a passing fad, while for Wordsworth, and others of like mind, it was the railway's despoliation of the landscape that caused despair. Despite their views, the train had come to stay. As the power house of industry and the engine of social change, the railway was unstoppable, and its tentacles spread rapidly to almost every corner of Britain, becoming, for more than a century, an integral part of the British way of life. Now, after four decades of radical political and social change, its great days are gone and, in the uncertain climate of today, only the main lines seem to have a future. The country railway has become an endangered species, its rural routes threatened with extinction by the policy of privatization. However, the practical reality of the country railway's steady decline has been marked by an extraordinary outburst of enthusiasm and nostalgia: not for the real thing, however, which lingers away largely unloved, but for the fantasy of the country railway of the 'good old days' that has been created all over Britain by the railway preservation movement. This book explores both the real country railway, struggling to survive against the odds, and the preserved version, a nostalgic journey of the imagination.

Between the 1840s and the end of Queen Victoria's reign at the very beginning of the twentieth century, the surface of Britain was covered with an intricate network of railways. These railways served not only every city and large town, but also almost every small town and a surprising numbers of villages and hamlets. Few places in Britain were far from a station, the railway having conquered even the remote heartlands of Wales and the hitherto inaccessible Highlands of Scotland. The result was a social and an economic revolution that changed forever patterns of life in Britain that had been largely unaltered since the Middle Ages. Universal mobility, the massive development of trade and industry and the growth of tourism were the most obvious and direct benefits of what was probably the greatest creation of the entire Victorian age. The railways also imposed themselves upon the landscape of Britain in a dramatic way, and their embankments, cuttings, tunnels and bridges were built with a sense of scale worthy of the Romans, or the fantasies of Piranesi. Even the most remote corners were changed forever by those great armies of navvies recruited to build the lines, their progress rarely hindered by climate, terrain or social pressure. At the same time, the railways created a distinct style of architecture, modern, decorative, ambitious, yet with strong awareness of local traditions and materials. In their own way the railway builders contributed more to the making of the British landscape than even the masons of the Middle Ages. The visible legacy of the railway age remains all over the country for, even when the lines have been abandoned, their physical presence is still there, marked forever upon the landscape.

Much of Britain's railway network was built by hundreds of small and independent companies, inspired most often by essentially local needs and financed by local investors, industrialists and landowners. The great main lines, laid down from the late 1830s and conceived on a national scale, formed the basic core. It was the efforts of the small companies, however, that created in a rather piecemeal and unplanned fashion the complicated network of lesser lines that gave Britain, for the first time, a proper public transport system. Inevitably, there was plenty of duplication born out of competition, and there were many lines that never fulfilled the hopes of their shareholders, but the net result was a remarkably comprehensive national railway. Through the latter half of the nineteenth century, these small companies gradually merged together, or were absorbed by larger rivals, and by the First World War the railways of Britain were under the control of a number of large and generally well-known companies. These included the Great Western, the Great Eastern, the Great Northern, the London & South Western, the London & North Western, the South Eastern, the

Caledonian and the North British. In 1923, all the railways of Britain were grouped together to form the 'Big Four' – the Great Western, the Southern, the London, Midland & Scottish and the London & North Eastern. These companies ran the railways until the whole network was nationalized in 1948.

Throughout this long process of rationalization, the national network was largely unaltered and there were few closures, even in the furthest, least accessible and most uneconomic corners. The railway was firmly established at the heart of both national and local life, and whole regions, as well as small towns and villages, were dependent on their train services. Everyone and everything travelled by train, and the train was the backbone of both the national and the local economy. This pattern remained unchanged until the late 1950s, when the railway's hold on the economic and social heart of the nation began to be challenged by the dramatic growth of commercial, industrial and private road transport. Traffic of all types left the railways at an alarming rate. The response of the railways was rapid and radical. Over the next ten years, half of Britain's railway network simply disappeared under the national rationalization programme masterminded by Dr Beeching. The main targets were the secondary and country routes, then deemed to be irrevocably uneconomic and ruthlessly pruned as a result. Large areas of Britain lost its railways. The closure programmes affected not only the lines, but also the whole railway infrastructure: staff were axed and stations closed, and the local goods services completely died. The traditional image of the country railway fulfilling, with its leisurely services, friendly staff and flower-decked stations, a vital social need seemed about to be forever destroyed. The effect was devastating, particularly on those remote communities for whom road transport was simply not a viable alternative. A key philosophy behind the building of the railways in the nineteenth century had been the establishment of a universally accessible public transport system. This concept was cast aside, often in the interests of political expediency and short-term financial gain.

The response was rapid and unexpected. While there was a general, if reluctant, acceptance of the new dependence on road transport, the public expressed its attachment to the old railways through campaigns against closures, through a massive outburst of nostalgia on a national scale, and through the launch of the railway preservation movement. Practically every line closure of the 1960s and 1970s resulted in a preservation battle. Most were lost, but a surprising number were successful, and all over Britain small, privately owned and volunteer-operated railways began to appear. The emphasis was on the steam engine, itself an endangered species having been finally withdrawn from the British Railways network in 1968. The aim was not to supply a service, but to open a railway for the enthusiast and the tourist that re-created some perceived golden age of train travel. As a result, many preserved railways exist as a type of museum or entertainment centre, with a length of of track going nowhere in particular, and make no attempt to operate a viable transport system. The point is always the journey, not the getting there. As an exercise in applied nostalgia, the preserved railway has been remarkably successful. The steam engine is now flourishing and, rather than being at the very edge of extinction, the numbers being brought back to life seem to increase each year. Today, there are well over a hundred preserved lines, railway centres and museums scattered across the map of Britain, and they have become a major component in Britain's ever-growing and vitally important heritage business.

The success of the preservation movement has altered significantly the public perception of the country railway, turning it from a transport service into an entertainment fantasy. This has made it far harder for that public to appreciate those real rural railways that still survive on the fringes of the modern network. A surprising number of secondary routes and branch lines did survive the Beeching axe, sometimes for political reasons and sometimes because of public pressure and genuine local need, and these now offer, in leisure terms, some of the best railway journeys in Britain. More important, they also offer practical public transport. The problem is that, overshadowed by the preserved lines that have redefined in the public mind the function of a railway, they are under-used, expensive to operate and, in the current political climate, face a very uncertain future. It is quite possible that the railway map of Britain in the near future will include only the expensive main lines and a plethora of preserved lines – the equivalent of the zoo or the wildlife park.

In many parts of Britain, from Cornwall to the very north of Scotland, the real country railway is still alive, if not actually very well. Rural routes through richly varied and often spectacular landscape, and with attractive stations and other traditional structures, friendly staff and leisurely journeys are all still there to be enjoyed. By modern accounting methods they may be economically unviable, and certainly unappealing candidates for privatization, yet these lines are often vital for the communities they serve, historically important, and essential for any realistic public transport network in the future. Their real qualities are the journeys they offer. Unlike the preserved lines, it is the getting there that counts, even though the journey may also be a pleasure. Unlike the preserved lines, the trains are unimportant. They are simply practical modern vehicles that do not vary greatly from line to line, or from region to region. This book is a record of some of these real country railways, showing the lines as components in the landscape, as living history and as part of the social structure of rural Britain. Included as well are a number of preserved lines, to show their diversity and their particular appeal, with the emphasis on those that try to offer more than just an entertaining escape into nostalgia and fantasy.

The West Country

St Erth to St Ives

Opened in the 1870s by the Great Western Railway, the St Ives branch played a part in the development of the town and its coastline as a holiday centre. In order to encourage traffic, the GWR bought the eighteenth-century Tregenna Castle Hotel in the town in 1878 – an early example of railways going into the country hotel business – and until the 1950s through carriages from Paddington were a regular feature of the line during the summer season. In those days, there was a busy station, complete with buildings and plenty of sidings to handle the traffic. This site is now buried beneath the car park in the centre of the picture. The modern station is simply a platform and a set of buffers, and the train is just a couple of carriages shuttling to and fro, but the magic lives on. The crowds on the platform shows how popular the line still is, thanks to the weather and the successful park and ride system operated from Lelant. The new Tate Gallery at St Ives helps to fill the trains out of season.

T he West Country is the last significant habitat of that endangered railway species, the rural branch line. For decades, such lines were the social and economic underpinning of rural life, and their ribbons of rail reached into almost every corner of the country. However, widespread decimation during the closures of the 1960s and 1970s brought the branch line to the verge of extinction, except in the West Country. Its survival there is due largely to accidents of geography and history. Devon and Cornwall form a long peninsula that narrows steadily as it reaches out into the Atlantic. In railway terms, this meant a main line running the length of the peninsula to Penzance, a backbone from which spurs, or branches, were built to serve other parts of the region. A brief glance at any pre-war railway map will show this clearly, with the West Country covered by a complex network of branches and secondary routes, built mostly to serve the local ports, harbours and holiday resorts. Many of these have subsequently been swept away, but enough remains to give modern travellers the rare experience of branch line travel. In Cornwall, the traveller can step down from the thundering London express, for example, at Liskeard, Par, Truro or St Erth, and find a local branch line train waiting in a bay platform, ready for a leisurely journey to some quiet country terminus beside the sea.

Railways came early to the West Country, inspired by the need to transport copper and tin ore and other minerals from the mines and quarries to the coastal ports. The first locomotive-hauled line was the Bodmin & Wadebridge, opened in 1834, and this was followed by a number of others in the 1830s, including the Hayle Railway. Passengers were also carried on some of these early lines. Meanwhile, Brunel's Great Western Railway had reached Bristol in 1841, and this was the starting point for the rapid expansion of the West Country network. Lines were soon opened to Exeter and Plymouth, and in 1859, Brunel's bridge over the Tamar at Saltash was finally completed, the final link in the chain of

St Erth to St Ives

The St Ives branch leaves the main line at St Erth, not far from Penzance, and then runs along almost entirely beside the sea. The views are continuously delightful, first across the tidal estuary towards Hayle, and then over a series of sandy bays from the train's route along the cliffs. After Carbis Bay, where there is a small halt, St Ives comes into view, colourful houses curving steeply above the harbour. Near Lelant the line crosses the golf links, seen here in lovely evening light, with a distant view of Black Cliff and the dunes of the Towans. In the far distance, and visible almost throughout the entire journey, is Godrevy Point and its lighthouse.

railways that allowed trains to run between London and Penzance. Competition soon appeared in the form of the GWR's great rival, the London & South Western Railway, offering a different route to Exeter and Plymouth from London, and the steady development of a network of lines serving north Devon and north Cornwall. The late Victorian period and the early decades of this century witnessed the rapid growth of tourism in the West Country, much of which was inspired by the railways. Lines were built to serve the new resorts, such as Bude, Padstow, Ilfracombe, St Ives, Newquay, along with those already established, such as Torquay, Sidmouth and Lyme Regis, and the railway companies' efficient, modern advertising created new holiday centres, such as the Cornish Riviera and the Atlantic Coast.

Today, patterns of holiday making have changed dramatically, and many of the railways have gone, along with the industries and the resorts they once supported. However, enough still survives in the West Country to maintain the traditions of the real country branch line and to offer a new generation of travellers the rare pleasure of a delightful journey through the countryside to the sea.

Plymouth to Gunnislake

Old signal and point levers in the signal box at Bere Ferrers, traditionally colour-coded, hint at the nature of the old-fashioned branch line from Plymouth to Gunnislake. This line, itself an unexpected survival, is a fragment of a railway network of historical complexity and former importance. It all started in 1863, when the Tamar, Kit Hill & Callington Railway started to build a narrow-gauge line to link quarries in the region with Calstock quay on the Tamar, via an inclined plane. This company went bankrupt in 1869 and its uncompleted route was taken over and finished by the Callington & Calstock Railway, which, in turn, became the East Cornwall Mineral Railway. This line carried on in splendid isolation until the late 1880s, when it was bought up by the extravagantly named Plymouth, Devonport & South Western Junction Railway. It was converted to standard gauge and then connected, in the early 1900s, to its main line via its subsidiary, the Bere Alston & Calstock Railway.

Plymouth to Gunnislake

The weather-boarded signal box at Bere Ferrers, formerly known as Beer Ferris, is preserved as an example of a once universal but now increasingly rare railway structure. Sited on what is today a rather pleasant but little known branch line, the box formerly served a busy part of the Southern Railway's main line. The line ran to Plymouth via Exeter, Okehampton and Tavistock, much of which was closed in the 1960s. It is hard today, in what has became a delightful railway backwater, to imagine great expresses to and from London pounding past. To the north is Bere Alston, where there was the former junction with the Callington branch, whose complicated history is described opposite. With the main line running northwards now just a dim memory, it is a quirk of history that the old branch line has survived, at least as far as Gunnislake.

Plymouth to Gunnislake

Although it was a late addition to the landscape, not being opened until 1908, the Calstock viaduct is a fine example of this type of railway structure. Its 12 tall arches carry the single track across the Tamar, more than 100 feet above the water, with a notable elegance underlined by the delicacy of both its design and its setting. One of the last of Britain's great viaducts in the classic tradition of the nineteenth century, it was built to link the independent mineral lines west of the Tamar with the main line of the Plymouth, Devonport & South Western Junction line. Apparently built of stone, the viaduct is actually made of more than 11,000 concrete blocks, cast on site and jointed to look like stone – a pioneering use of this material.

Plymouth to Gunnislake

The route of the Gunnislake branch, once it has escaped the lingering suburbs of Plymouth and Devonport, is full of interest. It passes beneath Brunel's great bridge across the Tamar at Saltash, and then follows the river, climbing steadily into the hills that surround the Tamar valley. It was these hills, and the stones they contained, that inspired the building of the railway in the first place. At Bere Alston, the line turns west, on to what was the old Callington branch. It then emerges from the hills high above the river at Calstock, which is crossed on a high viaduct, a typically splendid piece of railway engineering, and unexpectedly grand on so minor a line. Visually exciting, and often dominating its environment, as in this case, the viaduct is the most evocative memorial to the skills and ambitions of the railway builders.

The Paignton & Dartmouth Steam Railway

The Paignton & Dartmouth Steam Railway took over the line between Paignton and Kingswear in the early 1970s, and since then has operated a passenger service in the classic style of the old Great Western Railway. Opened in 1864 by the Dartmouth & Torbay Railway, and subsequently part of the Great Western's empire, the line has always catered for the needs of visitors wanting to enjoy the sandy beaches of Torbay and the particular qualities of the Dart valley. Today, the line's steam trains maintain this tradition, and offer a vital link between the mainline network at Paignton and the ferries that link Kingswear with Dartmouth. Consciously evocative in its style of an ill-defined golden era of railway travel, the line's trains and structures seem to belong in the 1920s or 1930s. Typical in its sense of period is the timber station at Kingswear, where it is all too easy to imagine the arrival of characters from an Agatha Christie novel, or even the author herself on her way to her house nearby.

Liskeard to Looe

In 1901 a line was built to link the mineral railways of the Looe valley with the Great Western's main line at Liskeard. Starting from a quite separate, and rather pretty wooden station, the line descends steeply, curving through the woods and passing beneath the main line, to join the old Liskeard & Looe line at Coombe junction. The layout of this still requires some delightfully archaic railway activity. In the picture, the train from Looe is approaching the junction. The guard, having donned his yellow safety jacket, has got down to operate the points, which he will change once the train has passed by. The train then sets off in the other direction, to start the final steep climb up to Liskeard, having paused to let the guard climb back on board. This procedure is a feature of every journey on the Looe branch.

Liskeard to Looe

The first practical link between the port of Looe, in south Cornwall and the market town of Liskeard, seven miles inland at the head of the East Looe river, was a canal. It was built largely for the carriage inland of sand, then used by farmers as a fertilizer. In about 1828, the canal company turned itself into a railway, building a horse-operated line along the route of the old canal. Some time later, this was linked to the Liskeard & Caradon Railway, a mineral-carrying line built in the 1840s to serve local clay pits. There were no passenger services, but in those days passengers could travel free in the mineral wagons, provided that they had a parcel or some object that did require a ticket. The line to Looe follows the river closely, and in places the bed of the old canal can still be seen, with some bridges and even a lock or two. Sandplace, the tidal head of the river, is where the old sand barges were loaded, and from here the line is right beside the broadening estuary.

Liskeard to Looe

Britain's real country railways, as opposed to its preserved lines, are still decorated with a wide variety of structures, pieces of equipment and signs surviving from an earlier era, and the pleasure of the journey can often be increased by looking out for these. There are still plenty of old signals to be seen, although they are disappearing quite fast, and old wooden signs saying Whistle or SW (short whistle) can occasionally be spotted. More common are the old speed-restriction signs, with their cut-out iron numbers in faded yellow paint. This example is on the branch line from Liskeard to Looe, in Cornwall.

Liskeard to Looe

The railway approaches Looe on a low embankment right by the water's edge, below the valley's steeply wooded western side. For passengers, it is a scene of seagulls, waders at low tide, fishing boats and yachts, and full of interest at any time of year. Looe station, a rather unremarkable structure well outside the town, is on the far right of this photograph. Originally, the line continued into the town to serve the harbour, whose quay was once busy with ships loading the clay brought down in railway wagons from the pits around Moorswater. In scenic terms, the Looe branch line is one of the best in Britain. The last few miles, along the tidal estuary, are a delight. The first few, south from Liskeard, are completely different, the line winding its way along a secret valley filled with flowers.

Liskeard to Looe

A little way beyond Coombe junction is Coombe station, a tiny halt dwarfed by the great stone arches of the viaduct carrying the main line. This is where the train pauses while the guard operates the points. The line that continues onwards to pass beneath the viaduct serves the still active china pits around Moorswater, and it is part of a once extensive network of mineral lines linked to the clay industry. Built by the Liskeard & Caradon Railway in the 1840s, this ran originally from Moorswater to South Caradon and Cheesewring. The huge Cornish clay deposits were the inspiration behind the building of many of the railways in the county, with many lines installed to link the pits with the harbours, in spite of the difficulties of the terrain. This is still a major industry, and is the lifeblood of much of the Cornish railway network. In the old days, many harbours played their part, including Looe, but now the industry is centred around St Austell, and the ports at Par and Fowey.

Bodmin & Wenford Railway

The Bodmin & Wadebridge Railway, Cornwall's earliest locomotive-operated line, opened in 1832, primarily for the carriage of stone and clay from Wenford Bridge and the moorland quarries to the harbour on the Camel estuary at Wadebridge. It remained in splendid isolation until 1887, when the Great Western opened a short branch to connect Bodmin with Bodmin Road, its existing mainline station four miles to the south. During the Beeching era, the railways of north Cornwall were progressively closed, but the line to Bodmin survived until 1983, kept open by the clay trains from Wenford Bridge. This was despite the fact that passenger services had ceased years before. Since then, the line from Bodmin Road to Bodmin has been reopened by the ambitious Bodmin & Wenford Railway. The sight of the steam trains blasting their way along the steeply graded route has become a regular feature of the summer season. It is a pretty journey along a line flanked by woods and flowers.

Bodmin & Wenford Railway

Resting between journeys up and down the Bodmin & Wenford's short route between Bodmin and Bodmin Road, the driver and the fireman pose for the camera by their gleaming tank locomotive. It is a classic railway scene, with many precedents from earlier decades, and it is a reflection of the excitement and pride that still surrounds that most personal of machines, the railway locomotive. It is a study in happy retirement, an old engine saved from the scrap heap and enjoying a new lease of life, and the elderly crew who, perhaps after many years of the hard reality of working for British Railways, cannot conceal their pleasure at being back on the footplate once more. Retired railwaymen are the backbone of the preserved lines, along with their old machines, representing a vital legacy of knowledge and experience.

Bodmin & Wenford Railway

Nostalgia is the key to the enduring popularity of the preserved railway, with trains and their surroundings carefully presented as things used to be or, rather, as things are now perceived to have been. It is all a delightful fantasy. Old stations, often pretty buildings in their own way, set the scene. Bodmin General, the Great Western's former terminus station just outside the town centre, and now the headquarters of the Bodmin & Wenford Railway, feeds the fantasy with its rough walls of local stone, its flowers and, most important of all, its scattering of old, enamel signs.

Exeter to Barnstaple

Stations on real country railways are sometimes just as good as the re-creations of the preserved lines. There is a particular quality to railway architecture, with its blend of Victorian historicism and vernacular tradition. The longest branch line in the West Country links Exeter and Barnstaple, a line that is notable for the quality of its landscape, its fine stations and its general air of being a survivor from another time. In the old days, what now operates as a branch line was a busy part of an extensive network of lines linking Exeter with Plymouth as well as large areas of Devon and north Cornwall. The great expresses from London would thunder through, bound for Bideford or Ilfracombe, Bude or Padstow. Unfortunately, all that is just a memory, and the scene shown here is Umberleigh station on a typically quiet day, a stone structure in the Tudor style characteristic of the line, and with nobody to enjoy the flower bed and the old gradient post.

Exeter to Barnstaple

The railway from Exeter to Barnstaple is now called the Tarka Line, after Henry Williamson's famous otter. The name is perhaps more than just a marketing ploy, for Williamson was a local man, and the line follows the Taw valley, the setting for Tarka's adventures. Historically, the line is interesting and quite early. It was built piecemeal in the 1850s, the first part by the Exeter & Crediton Railway and then the rest by the North Devon Railway & Dock Company. In the mid 1860s, it all became part of the burgeoning network of the London & South Western company, the GWR's great rival for West Country traffic. Today, it is just a long branch line, and the ubiquitous diesel railcars that shuttle to and fro give passengers ample opportunity for a leisurely enjoyment of the wooded hills and green fields of the Taw valley. Here, on a quiet summer's day north of Portsmouth Arms station, the cows are expecting rain, or perhaps just resting from the heat.

Exeter to Barnstaple

Framed by typical Devon hills turned golden brown by weeks of sun, an evening train rushes past Eggesford church on its way to Barnstaple. Famous for its monuments and its delightful setting beside the river Taw, the church is one of the many quiet delights of the Exeter to Barnstaple line, a real country railway that still serves the quite isolated communities along its route. It also offers by far the best way to see and to enjoy the varied landscape of the Taw valley, its churches, villages, country houses and old-fashioned stations, all of which are the essential components of a traditional English railway journey.

The South

The Swanage Railway

Beneath the battered pinnacles of Corfe Castle, the pride of the Swanage Railway's fleet, distinctive with its chunky streamlining in Southern Railway green, hauls its train southwards towards Swanage. Despite the timeless quality of this scene, the train actually came quite late to the Isle of Purbeck, and it was not until 1885 that the London & South Western Railway completed its branch line from Wareham to Swanage. This was a tourist route *par excellence* and, until its closure in the 1960s, holiday expresses from Waterloo pounded across Purbeck to serve the Isle's resorts and sandy beaches. Out of season, it became a real country railway, with leisurely services and the occasional goods train. After closure, the trackbed was quickly absorbed back into the landscape, and it is only through the efforts of the Swanage Railway that this memorable scene can once again be enjoyed.

In the nineteenth century the railway took southern England by storm, and the landscape was quickly taken over by a complex network of lines radiating out from London. Intercompany rivalry was bitter, resulting in the duplication of many routes, and ensuring that few places were far from a railway station. The major main lines, to Southampton, Brighton and Dover, were all in use by 1844, and others quickly followed, often inspired by the needs of a new generation of commuters who demanded rapid transport to and from the capital. The result of the proliferation of lines that followed was the development of the suburbs and the rapid expansion of many country towns and villages, whose quiet lives had been largely unchanged during previous centuries. The Home Counties around London were the heartland of this transport revolution, but nowhere was unaffected as the lines spread into the quiet corners of Dorset, Wiltshire, Hampshire, Sussex and the Kent coast and over the Isle of Wight. Most of the development was by the major companies – the Great Western, the London & South Western, and those great rivals in the south east, the London, Brighton & South Coast, the London, Chatham & Dover and the South Eastern. All of these finally came together in 1923 to form the Southern Railway. In its day this company, which operated both a massive commuter network and some of the most glamorous named expresses in Britain with considerable style, was among the best known in Britain. For millions the Southern meant green-painted electric trains to the suburbs, rural branch lines, holiday expresses hauled by distinctive locomotives, and those perennial favourites, the Brighton Belle and the Golden Arrow. However, many small, independent companies also played their part, particularly in the building of the more rural routes, and their names, often long forgotten, are dimly recorded in the annals of railway history. It was these lines that bore the brunt of the cuts and closures in the 1960s and 1970s, and so the real country railway is quite a rarity in the south of England. Classic cross-country lines do survive, such as those from Weymouth to Bath and from Hastings to Rye and Ashford, and they offer all the traditional pleasures of a leisurely exploration of England's varied landscape and quieter places.

An idealized version of the country railway is also offered by the many preserved lines in the south. The preservation movement has strong roots in this region, with some important pioneers who set the steam and preserved railway standard. There is now a huge choice of steam railways, railway centres and museums to tempt and delight the visitor. Many of these offer only the predictable escape into nostalgia and fantasy, something that can be entertaining as well as educational, even though it has little to do with the social and economic reality of the country railway. Others, such as the famous Romney, Hythe & Dymchurch Railway, manage to combine and balance nostalgia with a traditional approach to public service. The Isle of Wight, always a microcosm of railway development in the south of England, still has a real country railway lingering on, a preserved steam line, and a whole network of abandoned routes to be explored on foot or by bicycle.

The Swanage Railway

Resting in its suitably soot-begrimed shed, an old Southern Railway tank engine enjoys a new lease of life with the Swanage Railway. In front of the shed is the turntable, that once universal symbol of the steam age. The Swanage Railway is the classic preservation story, with the dreams of enthusiasts and volunteers being gradually turned into a reality as the long process of rebuilding has brought the line back to life. It all started in Swanage, where the old station still survived, and from here the line was relaid, in stages and painstakingly slowly. In 1995 it reached Corfe Castle, where there is a new station and park-and-ride facility, to underline the fact the preserved railways are not just toys, but can also serve their communities. Not far north of Corfe, the old line still exists, in use as a freight link to the Wych Farm oil installation. The Swanage Railway's ambition is to rebuild its line to this point, and then run its trains once again into Wareham's Flemish-style station.

Weymouth to Bristol

With the landscape showing the remarkable colours of a long, hot summer, the valley of the river Avon winds southwards from Bath. The Kennet and Avon Canal, hidden by the trees, follows the valley prior to its river crossing on Rennie's wonderful Dundas aqueduct, a classical masterpiece in honey-coloured Bath stone. Closer to the river, and hugging its curves, is the line of the railway from Bath to Weymouth, a rural route notable for its rich variety of landscape. The first section, south from Bath, is along the Avon valley. A quieter stretch then carries it across Wiltshire farmland and the flat lands of Somerset, before the final assault on the hills of Dorset. It carves its way through a landscape still charged with the spirit of Thomas Hardy, and marked by the great earthworks of prehistory. The end of the line is at the seaside – the perfect finish for any railway journey.

Weymouth to Bristol

This view southwards from Chetnole is typically Dorset, seen at its best from the train. When the line opened in 1857, after a long and rather tortuous period of construction, it made accessible a traditional part of England virtually unchanged since the Middle Ages. The spirit of those days lives on, in the names of villages and hills, and in the pleasure of a journey through an ancient landscape. The grandly named Wiltshire, Somerset & Weymouth Railway began to build the line in 1845, with the backing of the Great Western, which had its eyes on Weymouth harbour and the potential of shipping services to France and the Channel Islands. Slow progress led the GWR to take control in 1851, and so the line was built originally to Brunel's famous broad gauge, which was not converted to standard gauge until 1874. Today, the line is a wonderful country railway, and still a valuable link between Bristol and Bath and the south coast.

Isle of Wight Steam Railway

The first railway in the Isle of Wight was opened in 1862, between Cowes and Newport. This grew into a flourishing network operated originally by a number of independent companies that served almost every corner of the island. Always steam-hauled, and a perfect example of the country railway, even during its last years under the control of British Railways, the network was sorely missed after its closure. It was partly in response to this that the Isle of Wight Steam Railway came into being, and it has reopened the line between Wootton and Smallbrook Junction, where there is a junction with the modern Ryde to Shanklin service. In the picture here, the immaculately dressed guard relives the days of the old Southern Railway as he prepares his train of elderly, green-painted carriages for departure from Haven Street, which is the steam railway's headquarters.

Isle of Wight Steam Railway

When the Isle of Wight's railway network was finally closed down in the mid 1960s, the island lost one of its more idiosyncratic and entertaining features. However, for reasons now lost in the mists of time, one route was spared, that from Ryde to Shanklin. This was electrified and then reopened with services operated by retired London underground trains. Retained with the line was Ryde's decorative iron pier, complete with its dragon and gryphon brackets. This is now the only place in Britain where passengers can step straight from the ferry at the pierhead into a waiting train. The first promenade pier was opened in 1814, and a tramway ran along this from 1866. The present railway pier and the pierhead station, shown in the picture, were built in 1880, giving Ryde the luxury of having three stations – Pierhead, St John's and Esplanades – all of which survive today.

Isle of Wight Steam Railway

Only the guard's orange safety vest gives away the date of this typical Isle of Wight railway scene, near Smallbrook Junction. With the guard's green flag showing that the points are correctly set, the driver and fireman watch carefully as they reverse their old tank locomotive towards the waiting carriages. The aim behind the Isle of Wight Steam Railway has been to recapture the atmosphere and style of the island's train services during their heyday between the wars, and it has done this remarkably well.

Isle of Wight Steam Railway

The leisurely pace of railway life in the Isle of Wight meant that the network was often the final resting place for old locomotives and rolling stock exhausted by years of hard work elsewhere. Despite this, there were some locomotives that were very characteristic of the island. Notable was the fleet of Adams tank engines that became the mainstay of the network from the mid 1920s. Introduced by the Southern Railway after its formation in 1923, they had a special number sequence, prefixed by W for Wight, and most were named after towns and villages on the island. Some lived on until the final closure in 1966, including w24, Calbourne, whose cab side number plate is shown here. This engine is now in service with the Isle of Wight Steam Railway, and it is the only one of the class still in use today.

Mid-Hants Railway

In the old days, even though every country station was fully staffed and everyone had plenty to do, there were always times when not much was happening. It was at these times that station gardens were brought up to scratch and those staff photographs were taken, so evocative of the country railway in the Edwardian era. Today, stations on preserved railways are mostly staffed by volunteers, who have to work hard to keep everything spic and span in the continual battle with wear and tear and the elements. With no trains imminent and unexpectedly with no duties demanding his attention, the station master at Ropley on the Mid-Hants Railway snatches a rare quiet moment in the sunshine with his book.

Mid-Hants Railway

In 1865 the Mid-Hants Railway, formerly the Alton, Alresford & Winchester Railway, completed its short but heavily graded line. It then enjoyed an independent life for the next 15 years before being absorbed by the London & South Western company as part of an alternative route from London to Southampton. Never particularly busy, the line came into its own during the two world wars, since it offered a more direct link between garrisons in the Aldershot region and the south coast ports. Deemed an unnecessary duplication, it was closed in 1973, and then reopened from Alton to Alresford ten years later as the preserved Mid-Hants Railway. Steam trains, hauled by a variety of predominantly former Southern Railway locomotives, have made the line more popular than it ever was during its real life. Here, on a quiet summer's day, a typical Mid-Hants train drifts into Ropley station.

Mid-Hants Railway

Old railway colour schemes are still surprisingly familiar years after they went out of use. Everyone seems to know the chocolate and cream of the GWR, the maroon of the LMS, and the green and cream of the Southern. The Mid-Hants Railway's desire consciously to keep alive the spirit and style of the Southern Railway is reflected by the colours of Alresford station. Old posters, flower baskets and some distinctive barge-boarding fringing the platform canopy are all endearing period railway features whose lasting appeal is understandable.

Romney, Hythe & Dymchurch Railway

Opened in the late 1920s, the Romney, Hythe & Dymchurch Railway was the creation of two well-known racing drivers and railway enthusiasts who wanted a real railway, but only on a miniature scale. In spite of various ups and downs in the past, the 15-inch gauge line lives on, operated as a proper public-service railway serving a remote part of the Kent coast that now has no other rail links. Today, it operates school trains, as well as a full timetable to suit the needs of both local residents and visitors. In this respect, it is far more a real country railway than most of the preserved lines. When it was built, to the designs of Henry Greenly, it was modelled on the London & North Eastern Railway, thus its original fleet of steam locomotives was inspired by famous engines, such as the Flying Scotsman.

Romney, Hythe & Dymchurch Railway

The route of the Romney, Hythe & Dymchurch Railway runs beside the sea, at the fringes of the Romney Marsh, and the train is the best way to explore this very distinctive coastal landscape. Its southern terminus, just by Dungeness's miles of shingle beach, was originally a wild and remote spot, with just a few old chalets and the famous lighthouse. Now all this is dwarfed by the huge buildings of the nuclear power station, which, itself, makes a contribution to an already extraordinary landscape. In this setting, the diesel-hauled train travels around the long turning loop before setting off back along the coast towards Hythe.

Hastings to Ashford

The best part of the journey between Hastings and Ashford is the section from Winchelsea to Appledore. It first runs through farmland and then across the vast expanses of Walland and Romney Marsh, with distant views of Winchelsea, the ruins of Camber Castle and the lighthouse at Dungeness. In the mid nineteenth century, many of the railways fought to capture the most lucrative routes between London and the south coast, with the two greatest rivals being the South Eastern Railway and the London, Chatham & Dover Railway. Many secondary routes, such as the Hastings to Ashford line, were created, or absorbed, in the process of these and similar battles. Those that survive today represent some of the best of Britain's country railways.

Hastings to Ashford

It is still possible to visit much of the coastline of southern England by train, and there is no better way to enjoy the varied seaside landscape. Particularly memorable is the journey from Hastings to Ashford along the northern fringes of Romney Marsh. It is a curiously remote route, with several of its stations, notably Winchelsea and Appledore, well away from the towns they serve. It is a journey of huge skies and magnificent views across the marsh and farmlands towards the sea.

Hastings to Ashford

At the heart of the Hastings to Ashford route is Rye, and from the train there are fine views of the town, its harbour and the tidal estuary of the river Rother. Another famous feature of the route is the windmill, seen here as the train approaches the station through an old-fashioned clutter of signs, sheds and equipment. The train is diesel-powered, since this secondary route had never been electrified. Rye has a remarkable station, designed by William Tress for the South Eastern Railway in 1851, It has a formal, Italianate structure in the Florentine style, with a three-arched loggia, and a fine example of the the concern for architectural quality exhibited by many Victorian country stations.

East Anglia

Colchester to Sudbury

Chappel viaduct, whose 32 arches absorbed more than 7 million bricks when it was built in 1849 to the designs of Peter Bruff, is the major feature of the short branch line from Marks Tey, near Colchester, to Sudbury. It is a scenic journey, with part of its route along the valley of the Stour, and near by are two railway preservation centres – the East Anglian Railway Museum, at Chappel & Wakes Colne station, and the Colne Valley Railway, near Castle Hedingham on the former Colne Valley & Halstead Railway. The line to Sudbury is itself a fragment of a once far greater network, built from the late 1840s to link Colchester with Bury St Edmunds and Cambridge, initially by the grandly named Colchester, Stour Valley, Sudbury & Halstead Railway. All the rest was swept away in the 1960s, leaving just the delightful branch line to Sudbury.

The railways of East Anglia, although eventually brought together first by the Great Eastern Railway and subsequently under the huge umbrella of the LNER, were notable for their individuality, and for the many small companies that created them. Development of the network during the 1840s and 1850s was remarkably piecemeal. The companies involved included the Eastern Union, the Ipswich & Bury St Edmunds, the Eastern Counties, the Lynn & Ely, the Norfolk, the Yarmouth & Norwich, the Wells & Fakenham, the East Suffolk, and many, many more. Each company maintained a firm sense of of its own individuality, especially for the styles of their stations and other railway structures. The result was, on the one hand, the eventual establishment of the major main lines and, on the other, the creation of a meandering network of predominantly rural lines reaching into almost every corner of the region, a network that remained virtually unchanged until the 1950s. Rivalry brought duplication and small towns, such as Aylsham or North Walsham, ended up endowed with two stations, built by different companies, and many small and previously isolated villages were also able to enjoy the benefits of the railway. Particularly well served were the major ports, such as Lowestoft, Yarmouth and Ipswich, and the little local harbours, such as Wells, Aldeburgh, Snape, Brightlingsea and Maldon.

The widespread distribution of the railway was encouraged by the relative flatness of the landscape. There were few engineering features of note in the region, apart from some viaducts, swing bridges over the navigable rivers, and hundreds of level crossings, which are one of the most characteristic features of the railway network of East Anglia.

Railways were, therefore, relatively cheap to build, and could afford to exist primarily on the carriage of passengers and a wide range of livestock and agricultural produce. Fish was an important staple of the freight business and this traffic encouraged the massive expansion of Lowestoft and Yarmouth. Tourism

Colchester to Sudbury

The glorious landscape of the Sudbury branch, and of the Stour valley in particular, is the landscape known by John Constable, and it is sometimes possible to see echoes of his paintings in the views from the carriage window. It is a country dominated by huge East Anglian skies over traditional farms, woodland and river valleys, with the gentle hills etched with a pattern of fields and hedgerows. In this late-summer view in the Stour valley south of Sudbury, it is the train and the pylons that seem out of place. Constable did not live to see the railway's invasion of the Stour valley, and his favoured landscape of the borders of Essex and Suffolk. And it is probably just as well.

also played its important part, with the railways contributing significantly to the development of the resorts on the north Norfolk coast and the broads. The Royal Family also played a part, for Sandringham's popularity coincided with the opening up of the Norfolk coast by the railway. As a result, the railway routes of the East Anglia region continued to extend their presence well into this century, with the last lines being built in the early 1900s under the auspices of the grandly named Midland & Great Northern Joint Railway, which, despite its title and its elegant locomotives, was the country railway *par excellence* with a predominantly rural network that wandered across the remote corners of north Norfolk.

Despite the drastic pruning of the railways in the 1960s, East Anglia still offers the visitor a large choice of essentially country railways. Notable are the lines from Ipswich to Lowestoft, from Norwich to Sheringham and Yarmouth, and along the Stour valley to Sudbury. A few preserved lines add to the mixture, and reflect the sense of individuality and eccentricity that has always been a typical feature of the region. East Anglia has some wonderful country stations, not the least of which is Berney Arms, which is probably unique in Britain in being accessible only by train or boat.

Colchester to Sudbury

The low-lying landscape of East Anglia made railway building relatively simple and, by about the middle of the nineteenth century, many independent railway companies were laying their tracks across Essex, Suffolk and Norfolk. Common to all of them was a profusion of level crossings, dictated both by economy and by the nature of the landscape, and these are a particular feature of East Anglia even today. Originally, each level crossing was manned and had its own keeper's cottage. Many of these reflect the particular architectural style favoured by their builders, from cottage simplicity to classical complexity. Today, a level crossing, complete with a keeper's cottage and traditional gates, is a rare sight outside the sheltered world of the preserved railway. However, examples of these traditional structures can still be found as surviving elements of the country railway. This one lingers on near Bures station, on the Sudbury branch.

Ipswich to Lowestoft

There can be no more typical railway structure than the tall wooden-clad signal box, and it must be familiar to every child that has ever played with a train set. Yet, the rise of the computer and the modern electronic age has rendered the traditional signal box almost obsolete, and they are now on the point of disappearing in the real world. This fine example, set high to give the signalman a good view along the tracks under his control, is at Westerfield Junction, where the Felixstowe branch leaves the rural Ipswich to Lowestoft line. This is a busy spot because of the extensive container traffic flowing from Felixstowe docks. The branch was built in 1877, largely with freight in mind, by the independent Felixstowe Railway & Dock Company. The signalman also controls the issuing of tokens on the Lowestoft line, which is mostly single-track. The token system is a traditional method of ensuring that only one train can be on a stretch of track at any one time.

Ipswich to Lowestoft

The railways of East Anglia were built by a confusing plethora of independent companies, resulting in considerable duplication of route as they all jostled for territory. In the 1860s, they came together under the control of the Great Eastern Railway, who made sense of most of it. Typical was the line from Ipswich to Lowestoft, built largely by the East Suffolk Railway during the 1850s and forming, with its connections, an alternative route from Ipswich to Lowestoft, Yarmouth and Norwich. A surprising survival of the Beeching years, the line is now a delightful exploration of rural Suffolk, never far from the sea, via old market towns such as Woodbridge, Saxmundham and Beccles. It is a journey full of old-fashioned detail and attractive 'railwayana', and notable for its interesting stations. One of the best, as a building and because of its riverside site, is Woodbridge, whose typically decorative iron footbridge is shown here.

Ipswich to Lowestoft

Old railway buildings have a particular appeal, often made picturesque by gentle decay. There is a rich language of architecture and decorative detail to be enjoyed by those with an observant eye, and some of the best are, inevitably, to be found on the quieter country railways, where there is no real need to change things. Stations are obviously the best, and the most adventurous in architectural terms, but not to be overlooked are all the related structures that were once vital parts of the railway scene. At one time, almost every station had a goods shed, for the carriage of local freight was then as important as passengers. The service may have gone, but the buildings often linger on. This pretty timber-clad example, overgrown and still with an old paint scheme attractively distressed by time and weather, lurks uncared for by a siding at Westerfield.

Ipswich to Lowestoft

The ingenuity of Victorian railway engineers was considerable, and their legacy is a great variety of complex pieces of machinery, much of which is still in daily use. A common problem they had to surmount was a railway crossing a busy waterway on the level, and the answer was a swing or lift bridge. There were examples of these in East Anglia, made necessary by the low-lying landscape and the various river navigations of the region, and several survive, adding excitement to any journey. This particular bridge, which swings when necessary on its central support, carries the railway over the narrow stretch of water that separates Lake Lothing and Oulton Broad, near Lowestoft. The elderly wooden hut attached to its side, houses the bridge-keeper, and the red flag flies, warn boats to keep well clear.

Norwich to Sheringham

Traditional railway equipment is now normally a feature of the preserved railway, since it forms part of the conscious attempt to re-create the past. Probably nothing is quite as evocative as the old-fashioned signal, on its own or, as in this case, on a gantry to allow access for maintenance. In the old days, the gantry was also used when the lamps had to be lit at night. Behind is the old wooden signal box, with its array of levers to operate both signals and points by hand. This physically demanding operation has largely been made redundant by modern electronics, but plenty of old signals do still survive on Britain's country railways. While they do, so they add interest to the journey. This one is at Wroxham station, on the Norwich to Sheringham line in Norfolk.

Norwich to Sheringham

Until the 1960s, north Norfolk was very well served by the railways, with a network of lines largely created by two separate companies: the Great Eastern Railway and, that particular East Anglian phenomenon, the Midland & Great Northern Joint Railway. Today, all that remains, apart from some short stretches reopened as preserved lines, is the route from Norwich to Sheringham, via Wroxham, North Walsham and Cromer. This is a lovely journey to the dunes and beaches of the north Norfolk coast, across the broads and the open landscape, beneath a great expanse of sky. Typical is this distant view of the train in the country near Thorpe End crossing.

Norwich to Sheringham

Built as they were by often competing, independent companies, Norfolk's railways inevitably had some duplication of routes. This sometimes resulted in small towns, such as Cromer, Aylsham and North Walsham, having two stations. Norwich ended up with three stations – Victoria, Thorpe and City – all served originally by different railways. By the 1960s this had been reduced to two, and the Beeching axe removed most of the surviving network, along with Norwich City station. That left Thorpe, a handsome and impressive station in the French Renaissance style, designed in 1886 by Wilson and Ashbee for the Great Eastern Railway. Its most famous feature is the great dome, towering here above the muddle of power lines needed by the mainline services. Country trains, for Sheringham, Yarmouth and Lowestoft, generally leave from the little bay platforms on the right of this scene.

Norwich to Sheringham

Hidden away in the obscure corners of Britain's railway network are plenty of chance survivals from earlier, more decorative times. Old enamel signs in the colours of the great railway companies – green for the Southern, brown for the Great Western, maroon for the LMS, dark blue for the LNER, and pale blue for Scotland – have now mostly disappeared into the preserved railways, or the attics of collectors. Plenty of other things remain, however, to be spotted by sharp eyes, particularly if they are part of the fabric of a building. This old waiting room sign, in etched glass and probably dating from the beginning of this century, is still to be seen at North Walsham station, on the Norwich to Sheringham line.

Norwich to Sheringham

Bridges carrying railways are so common that nobody pays much attention to them. Yet, in their rich diversity, they also contribute much to the landscape, reflecting the dramatic changes that occurred when the railways were being built. Often made from local materials and respecting vernacular design traditions, these bridges can be both decorative and elegant. This substantial and handsome skew bridge, built out of the local soft, red brick, carries the Norwich to Sheringham line over a farm track near East Runton, where the train runs close to the sea. It reflects the care taken by those bygone railway engineers when they were designing even quite minor structures in the most out-of-the-way corners of the countryside. In remote spots, bridges often remain long after the lines they once carried have disappeared, representing picturesque memorials to the railway age.

North Norfolk Railway

Preserved railways are run mostly by volunteers, relying on the contribution made by retired or former railway employees for the smooth running of their operation. Many of the train crews have mainline experience, but equally as important is their enthusiasm and their desire to make their railway as good and as efficient as it possibly can be. These men, posing with pride on the platform at Weybourne station – are standing with their charge, an old former LNER tank engine, which looks spic and span and ready for action.

North Norfolk Railway

The North Norfolk Railway runs from Sheringham, along the coast for a few miles to Weybourne, and then turns inland to its terminus at the market town of Holt. Rescued in the aftermath of the line's closure in the 1960s and progressively reopened as a preserved steam railway, the North Norfolk keeps alive the traditions of the old LNER, and more particularly Norfolk's own railway – the Midland & Great Northern Joint. This rather idiosyncratic company, formed in 1893 from a number of smaller local concerns, operated a meandering 182-mile network of tracks over the northern half of the county. It was completely obliterated during the Beeching era, but this timeless picture shows that its memory lives on in the safe hands of the North Norfolk Railway.

North Norfolk Railway

With steam drifting into the trees, a North Norfolk Railway tank engine slowly hauls its train from Holt towards Weybourne station, where it passes beneath a smoke-stained road bridge. Weybourne was originally a small station, well away from its village and set on the edge of a large expanse of woodland. It is now the North Norfolk Railway's operations centre, and there are large custom-built workshops where rolling stock, locomotives and equipment are all restored, repaired and maintained. Behind the station are the sidings, filled with old and battered railway relics, awaiting their turn in the workshops. This familiar preserved railway scene reflects the usual shortage of money and time, and the dependence on volunteers.

North Norfolk Railway

Sheringham now has two stations. The real one is a pretty building in two-tone brick. It is richly decorated with old enamel signs in LNER dark blue and old platform paraphernalia, and is the terminus of the North Norfolk Railway. It dates from 1887, when the line from Cromer to Melton Constable was completed by the Eastern & Midlands Railway. Across the road, where there used to be a level crossing, a basic platform and a set of buffers identify the other station, the end of the line for trains from Norwich. There could be no greater contrast. One in its decorative splendour represents the flourishing fantasy world of the preserved railway; the other shows all too clearly the straightened circumstances and insecure future of Britain's real country railways.

Wells & Walsingham Light Railway

The British are famous for their love of steam trains, and it is this above all else that has made the preservation movement so successful. There are few corners of Britain now without some type of steam railway. There can be no greater expression of this love than the tiny Wells & Walsingham Light Railway, entirely the creation of one man, Captain Francis. Here, surrounded by clouds of steam, he attends to the needs of the railway's only locomotive – a magnificent small-scale Garrett, which was built especially for the line. Resplendent in dark blue and polished brass, it is named Norfolk Hero, and it has on its nameplate a profile of Lord Nelson, who was very much a local man.

Wells & Walsingham Light Railway

Completed in 1857 by the Wells & Fakenham Railway was a short, nine-mile line between the two towns. Typical of so many small, predominantly local Victorian railway companies that were planned, built and funded by local interests, the W & F remained independent until 1862, when it was absorbed by the mighty Great Eastern. Never a busy line, it was finally closed in 1964. Rather unexpectedly, Walsingham station became a Greek Orthodox church. Part of the trackbed, between a spot south of Wells and another north of Walsingham, is now the province of the Wells & Walsingham Light Railway, a delightfully eccentric operation and the longest 10½-inch gauge railway in Britain. Here, in a typical north Norfolk landscape, complete with a grand medieval church, the line's only train makes its way along its little track.

The Midlands

Great Central Railway

The fascination with trains is a peculiarly British phenomenon, but it is clearly not one shared by dogs. This hound looks distinctly uninterested as its enthusiast owner discusses some arcane point of locomotive practice with the driver of a Great Central Railway engine waiting the signal to leave Loughborough Central station. The Great Central, a preserved railway that has effectively re-created a busy mainline atmosphere, has a remarkable collection of restored locomotives. They are all classics from the great days of steam, and represent the Big Four – the GWR, the SR, the LMS and the LNER. Period signs, plenty of flowers and a careful scattering of old crates and packages all help to add to the atmosphere. In the distance is the water tower, a vital component of the steam railway scene.

The development of the railway network that covers the middle of England was, inevitably, centred on the major industrial regions, whose rise to prominence in the nineteenth century coincided with the railway boom. Freight was the driving force, and the major companies – the London & North Western, the Midland, and the Great Northern – built their wealth, and their expanding networks, on the revenues gained by the carriage of coal, stone, iron ore and other minerals, and the products of the great areas of industry and manufacture. The main lines ran initially from north to south, but soon the major east-west routes across the country were also opened up. To these were added, in a more piecemeal fashion, the intricate network of minor, rural and branch lines that gradually brought the benefits of the railway age to every small town, and most villages, in the Midlands.

The landscape, highly varied across the country, made its own impact on the railway builders, and so there are many regional variations in both architectural and structural styles, as well as in the materials used. Tough engineering brick, which is generally blue-black or deep red in colour, was the favoured material and it is a characteristic feature of the major industrial areas of the Black Country, the Severn Valley and the Derbyshire, Leicestershire and Nottingham regions. Elsewhere, in Oxfordshire and the Cotswolds, in Northamptonshire, in Lincolnshire and Rutland and in the wilder parts of Derbyshire and Staffordshire, for example, the locally available stone was used, to create impressive structures that have always been in harmony with the landscape. This variation of material adds interest to the landscape, and watching the change from region to region is one of the pleasures of the journey. Another delight comes from the observation of buildings and other railway structures, for the continuous variation in detail and style these demonstrate underlines the pride and the individuality of all those small companies that were the initial creators of the railway network.

Stations have a particular appeal, and even the smallest wooden structure usually has some sense of style. In the Midlands, all the favoured architectural forms of the Victorian period are represented: timber-framed, Italianate, neo-Tudor, Flemish, Gothic revival, French Renaissance, Classical and many more besides, with some of the most adventurous occurring on lesser or country lines. Many of these are now little used and often the worse for wear, while others on preserved lines are lovingly cared for. Collectively they represent one of the greatest legacies of the railway age. There are many country railways in the Midlands, some of which have altered little since they were first built, while others are the truncated remains of once great industrial networks. Even today, after years of neglect, unpopularity and closure, the quieter railways, and particularly those that cross the country from east to west, are still the best way to enjoy the varied landscape of the heart of England. Also well represented in the Midlands are the preserved lines, with some classic journeys that bring to life the glorious past of the Great Western, the Midland and that ambitious late arrival on the railway map, the Great Central.

Great Central Railway

While many locomotive drivers and firemen working on the preserved lines can draw on their long years of experience of railway operation, which frequently stretch back to the era of steam on British Railways, there are exceptions. The lure of steam frequently crosses the conventional barriers of both age and sex, and the traditional overalls, grease-top cap and enamel tea mug cannot conceal the feminine qualities of this driver/ fireperson in the cab of a Great Central Railway locomotive, resting between duties at Loughborough Central station.

Great Central Railway

The Great Central, a late arrival on the railway scene, finally completed its main line to London in 1899. It grew out of the ambitions of a thriving railway and docks business in the north of England – the Manchester, Sheffield & Lincolnshire Railway. This company, which was to become the Great Central in 1893, was determined to have its own main line to London, almost regardless of cost, and it also had its eye on routes to Scotland and links to Europe via a channel tunnel. In the event, it arrived too late, and without sufficient funds, in an already overcrowded market. Thus, despite the elegance and efficiency of its trains, its independence was only short-lived and it was absorbed into the LNER in 1923. Much of its route was closed in the 1960s, including the section between Leicester and Loughborough, which has now been reopened and is operated by its preserved railway namesake. This is the original Loughborough Central station, at one time one of three in the town, and now the headquarters of the preserved line.

Bedford to Bletchley

In 1846 the Bedford Railway opened its line between Bedford and Bletchley. At that time, it was just a branch from George Stephenson's London & Birmingham Railway, which operated the line, but later it was extended westwards to Oxford and eastwards to Cambridge, becoming the main railway link between those towns. The original section from Bedford to Bletchley still survives, complete with a number of its remarkable timber-framed stations. Inspired by the designs in J C Loudon's famous book on cottage, farm and villa architecture, published in 1833, and built in a picturesque style to tone in with the Duke of Bedford's nearby estate at Woburn, these pretty buildings underline the architectural inventiveness of many early railway engineers. This is Millbrook, one of several similar stations that are the highlight of a journey on this particular country railway.

Bedford to Bletchley

Station architecture is delightfully varied, and its often unpredictable qualities can add greatly to the pleasures of a country railway journey. Many of the smaller stations did not warrant proper buildings on both sides of the track, and so there emerged a tradition of creating what are little more than decorative sheds – at first in wood and, later, in corrugated metal, concrete and other materials. Particularly famous is the pagoda style in corrugated metal favoured by the GWR during the 1930s. The basic structure shown here, made appealing by its decorative barge-board, is at Millbrook, on the Bedford to Bletchley line. Its simplicity balances the ornate picturesqueness of the main station building.

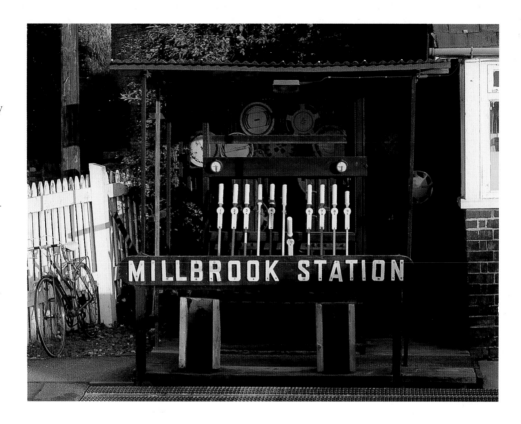

Bedford to Bletchley

A collection of hub caps and wheel trims – trophies in the continuing contest between railway and road – decorates the primitive shelter that houses the point and signal levers at Millbrook station. This is a genuine country railway scene, free from the sometimes excessively contrived and self-consciously old-fashioned atmosphere of the preserved lines. This is the real thing, an incidental accessory to decorate a rural journey, not a complex stage set, and all the more appealing for that.

Shrewsbury to Newport

The train journey through the Welsh Marches from Shrewsbury to Newport underlines the turbulent story of this border region as it passes the remains of several medieval castles, as well as the sites of a number of others that have long since disappeared. It is a journey of river valleys and green hills, richly decorated with the relics of history from Roman times to the nineteenth century. One of the highlights is the view of thirteenth-century Stokesay Castle. which stands, with its church, right beside the track near Craven Arms. This fortified mansion, set on the bank of the Onny river, was one of the first in England to bring together, in so clear a fashion, the needs of domestic life with a conventional defensive structure.

Shrewsbury to Newport

With the Gavenny river in the foreground, and in a setting of typical green hills, this view of the railway north of Abergavenny captures the predominantly rural atmosphere of the Shrewsbury to Newport line. Opened in 1854 as the Newport, Abergavenny & Hereford Railway, it first became part, in 1860, of the ambitious West Midland Railway, which, in turn, was absorbed by the Great Western three years later. With its many connections, most of which were closed years ago, the line was once a busy route to the Midlands and the North for the coal mines and industries of South Wales. Now, it is just a classic country railway running through a delightful sweep of landscape.

Shrewsbury to Newport

Early on a fine summer's morning, a typical two-coach local train travels along the Shrewsbury to Newport line near Abergavenny. In clear light the traditional patchwork of fields and hedgerows highlights the unchanging nature of the landscape. In the distance are the rounded shapes of the Black Mountains. As it follows a series of river valleys, the railway has an easy route through the surrounding hills, with no major engineering features, but with a continuous series of fine views from the train.

Shrewsbury to Newport

In the nineteenth century, the Shrewsbury to Hereford line was a type of railway lynch pin for the region, and its route was a series of junctions with lines radiating out to the east and west. Today, few of these exist, but Craven Arms, formerly one of the most important, still survives. Here, trains from Shrewsbury to Swansea, on the long route across the heart of Wale,s branch away to the south west. The buildings of the former Junction station also survive, but now enjoying a new lease of life as a tea shop. Redundant stations find many new uses and spotting these can add interest to any journey. Many have been converted into private houses, particularly those on closed lines. Restaurants and cafes are quite common, as are shops, with bookshops, hairdressers and even a pets parlour being typical.

Severn Valley Railway

This traditional, flower-bedecked station in the spirit of the old GWR, is Arley, on the Severn Valley Railway, one of Britain's best-known preserved lines. The original Severn Valley Railway was incorporated in 1853 and was completed nine years later, by which time it had been acquired by the West Midlands Railway. Later, it became a part of the Great Western's ever-expanding empire, and it was the GWR that added the link from Bewdley to Kidderminster in 1878, which is now a vital part of the preserved railway's popular 16-mile route to Bridgnorth. The Great Western, or God's Wonderful Railway as it was widely and affectionately known, was famous for its huge network of country lines in Wales and western England. It is the lasting memory of those services, as much as its famous high-speed express trains, that made the GWR so popular with modern railway enthusiasts.

Severn Valley Railway

The steam locomotive, that much-loved symbol of the railway age, came to the end of the line in Britain in 1968, when the last surviving examples were withdrawn by British Railways. Since then, most other countries in the world have followed suit, and so it is in practical terms an endangered species. However, the locomotive's disappearance from the main line was matched by the introduction and rapid growth of the preservation movement, and there are now about a hundred private railways, museums and railway centres in Britain flourishing on a popular tide of nostalgia. Most of these own and operate steam locomotives, and so several hundred are alive and well in Britain today, making available to the next generation the experience of the steam railway. Here, in the gleaming cab of a former Great Western locomotive now in service with the Severn Valley Railway, the roaring fire says all there is about the sight, sound and smell of a steam engine.

Severn Valley Railway

On a wet summer's day, with the fishermen beside the Severn below waiting for the fish to rise, an old Great Western locomotive, running tender first and blowing off clouds of steam, hauls its train across the Victoria Bridge. This well-known view, familiar from postcards, calendars and hundreds of books, captures the particular flavour of the Severn Valley Railway, a company whose trains, stations and general atmosphere helps to keep alive the memory of Britain's greatly lamented rural railway network.

Derby to Matlock

The 1840s was a frenetic period in the development of Britain's railway network. Among the many lines authorized by Parliament was the Manchester, Buxton, Matlock & Midland Junction Railway. This trans-Pennine route, supported by the Duke of Devonshire but condemned by John Ruskin, was to connect at Ambergate with the Nottingham, Erewash Valley & Ambergate Railway. After numerous difficulties – financial, physical and political – the route was finally completed nearly 20 years later, as one of the most attractive and exciting of the trans-Pennine lines. In 1968, Dr Beeching chopped out the centre section, leaving two disjointed, but still visually impressive branch lines – Manchester to Buxton and Derby to Matlock. In this picture, engineers carry out sonic testing of the track near Matlock, in a rock-lined cutting typical of the dramatic character of the line.

Derby to Matlock

In 1794, the Cromford Canal was completed, linking Cromford and the textile mills of the Derwent valley with the Erewash Canal at Langley Mill, and thus with the river Trent. Thirty years later, the first railway arrived – the Cromford & High Peak – famous for its steep gradients, inclined planes and rugged Pennine engineering. Another 30 years saw the completion of the line from Manchester to Derby via Buxton and Matlock, which closely followed the route of the canal along the narrow Derwent valley. It is seen here passing under the aqueduct that carries the canal over it near Cromford. Although the Cromford Canal was closed years ago, and parts of it abandoned, the northern section has been restored, along with the famous Leawood pumping house near this aqueduct, built to raise water to the canal from the river.

Derby to Matlock

It was the Midland Railway that finally pulled together all the loose strings and finished the line from Manchester to Derby via Buxton and Matlock. With its tunnels, viaducts, splendid Pennine scenery and the beautiful Derwent valley, it was a memorable route, now sadly truncated. Also impressive were many of the stations, notably Cromford with its fine stonework, French-style steeples, lattice windows and decorative ironwork. It was designed by G H Stokes, assistant to Sir Joseph Paxton at Chatsworth, and its individuality owes much to the Duke of Devonshire's stoic support for the railway. Luckily, despite the line's incomplete state and uncertain future, the delightful eccentricity of that and other buildings can still be enjoyed.

Manchester to Buxton

Buxton was a prize fought over by two railway companies, the Midland and the London & North Western, and their rival lines into the town opened within days of each. It was the Duke of Devonshire who insisted that they put aside their differences and have one shared station – and it may have been his architect, Sir Joseph Paxton, who designed it. The original station was in the form of two identical structures side by side, powerfully classical in rusticated stone, and each with a great fan window, one proudly inscribed *Midland Railway* and the other *London & North Western Railway*. Apparently, the two rivals held their opening dinners on the same night. The Duke went to one, the Midland's, while Paxton, ever diplomatic, attended both. Today, only one survives, a gaunt and sadly incomplete reminder of Victorian rivalries.

Manchester to Buxton

A minor farm track zigzags across a typical Derbyshire patchwork landscape of steeply sloping fields bounded by stone walls. This is the foot of Black Edge, north of Buxton, which rises to more than 1660 feet. The isolated building is part of Blackedge Farm, still made accessible only by the handsome stone accommodation bridge built by the railway in the 1860s. The pleasures of a railway journey across this kind of landscape are boundless, and it is remarkable that the little-used fringes of Britain's railway network can still offer such pleasures.

Manchester to Buxton

Three bridges in rusticated Derbyshire gritstone echo the tough nature of the Pennine landscape. This is Dove Holes station, north of Buxton, and the bridges underline the rugged architecture characteristic of the line from Manchester to Buxton. The most dramatic part of the journey was in the now closed section south of Buxton, through Miller's Dale and across the great Monsal Dale viaduct.

Peak Rail, an ambitious preservation venture, is trying to reopen all the line between Buxton and Matlock, and thus bring back to life this great trans-Pennine route. Beneath this station is a tunnel built by another company in the 1860s, a further reflection of the bitter railway battles of the Victorian era over routes linking Manchester with Derby and Nottingham.

Manchester to Buxton

Victorian railway rivalries resulted in there being two stations in Chapel-en-le-Frith, formerly called Central and South. Central vanished years ago, along with its railway, but South lingers on, almost hidden by the surrounding woodland. The views out across what the Victorians called Little Switzerland are spectacular, and their enjoyment of this Peak landscape encouraged them to build some of the stations, such as Matlock Bath, in a type of Swiss chalet style. This landscape imposed great demands on both the railway engineers and the navvies who built the lines. They have fitting memorials in the grand viaducts they built across the hills. Two stand at Chapel Milton, forming a great junction of stone arches just above the village. One was built in 1866, and then the other was added in 1893, to carry the Hope Valley line to Sheffield, the last of the three trans-Pennine railways in this area.

Wales

**Aberystwyth
to Pwllheli**

The few lines that remain
in Wales are true country
railways, the best of them
offering a slow and leisurely
exploration of the Welsh
landscape and coastline.
A feature of the coast is
the broad tidal estuaries,
and these posed problems for
railway builders. The largest is
the Dovey (Dyfi) estuary, and
the original plan to construct
a bridge across it proved
impracticable. As a result,
the line was built around
the estuary, crossing the river
on the long, low bridge seen
in this picture. It is a remote
and beautiful place, filled
with the cries of the birds
that crowd the mud flats
at low tide. Just beyond the
bridge is Dovey Junction
station, a bare and windswept
platform where the Cambrian
coastline from Aberystwyth
northwards to Pwllheli meets
the railway that runs inland
across Wales to Shrewsbury.

It is an irony that those regions of Britain most dependent on the railway were those most affected by the closures of the 1960s. Wales was probably hardest hit, and only a skeleton of lines survives today, a remnant of the complex network laboriously built up in the Victorian period to make accessible even the most hidden corners of the country. Wales was probably the natural home of the country railway, since its demanding landscape made, until recently, all other forms of transport impracticable. The inspiration was primarily industrial, and from the late eighteenth century primitive railways had been in use to move coal and stone from the mines and quarries to the coastal ports. In the south, coal mines and ironworks brought great prosperity to the railway and docks companies that masterminded the industrial development of the region while, in the north, slate was king, served by a number of small, narrow-gauge lines. The rest of Wales was, as far as the railway companies were concerned, a rural wilderness, and yet they drove their lines across the country and through the mountains, almost regardless of cost, inspired by the needs of local industries, agriculture and, increasingly, tourism. Small companies slowly put together a network of routes that made accessible the south west, the Cambrian coast, the heart of Wales and Snowdonia. They merged together to form larger companies, the most important of which was the Cambrian, and then eventually most came together under the control of the Great Western. Only the very north remained firmly the territory of the London & North Western, the GWR's great rival.

The railways brought wealth to Wales and they carried the country into the modern world. They opened up the country to tourism and developed the resorts of the south west and the north coast. Most important, they created an economic and social infrastructure on which the country came to depend.

Casually, almost mindlessly, the closure programme swept all that away, leaving large areas of the country without any real form of public transport. However,

Aberystwyth to Pwllheli

One of the great railway journeys of Britain is the line all along the coast of Wales from Aberystwyth to Pwllheli, a wonderful exploration of the country's coastal scenery. It was created by one company, the Aberysthwith (*sic*) & Welsh Coast Railway, which merged with Cambrian Railways shortly before the line's completion in 1867. Rarely far from the sea, and often virtually on the beach, the line is just a series of spectacular views as it follows the meandering coastline. Here, near Tonfanau, it crosses a typical landscape of small fields bordered by stone walls, with distant views of Barmouth and Snowdonia.

the lines that did survive, albeit precariously, notably along the Cambrian coast and across the heart of the country to Aberystwyth and Swansea, are now among the best of Britain's country railways. Long, leisurely and restful explorations of a country of spectacular landscape, they are still full of the echoes of the great days of the railway age.

The closure programme also brought a new importance to the remaining narrow-gauge lines. Two of these, the Talyllyn and the Ffestiniog, were early pioneers in preservation, becoming the launch pad for what is now a national movement. Other lines followed, some rescued and reopened, and some created from scratch, with the result that Wales has, over the last two decades, become the land of the Great Little Trains. The best of these are proper railways, playing their part in maintaining some type of transport infrastructure, and helping to encourage the tourism on which Wales increasingly depends.

Aberystwyth to Pwllheli

Near Llwyngwril the line was built at the water's edge, at the base of the cliffs. Falling rocks, often set off by the noise of the locomotive, caused great problems here, and a 4mph speed limit was imposed when the line was opened. Despite this, a landslide in 1883 swept an engine on to the beach. The driver and fireman were killed but the engine was recovered and repaired, and remained in service for another 30 years. After this there was a permanent watchman stationed by the line, and the Great Western, which took over in 1923, made improvements and raised the speed limit to 15 mph. In 1933 another landslide threw a second engine on to the beach, again killing its crew. After that, the company built the concrete avalanche shelter that still protects trains from the rocks that continue to fall at Friog. Not far ahead is Fairbourne's sandy peninsular, the long bridge over the estuary at Barmouth, and a distant view of Snowdon.

Snowdon Mountain Railway

During the late nineteenth century, north Wales enjoyed a tourist boom, and this encouraged the building of railways to make more accessible Snowdonia's landscape of mountains and river valleys. Typical was the Carnarvon & Llanberis Railway, whose nine-mile line to the foot of Snowdon was completed in 1869. This subsequently enjoyed a rather chequered career, and from the 1930s until its final closure in 1962 it was used only by summer excursion traffic. Many of those visitors arriving at Llanberis would have then transferred to the Snowdon Mountain Railway for the trip to the summit, and they would have been greeted by this familiar steam-age scene. On a wet and blustery summer's day, typical of the mountain's unpredictable weather, the fireman fills the locomotive's slab-sided water tanks. This is one of the railway's original Swiss-built engines that were delivered new in 1896.

Snowdon Mountain Railway

The Snowdon Mountain Railway completed its five-mile line to the mountain's summit in 1896. It is a dramatic journey, with gradients up to 1 in 5, made possible by the use of the Swiss Abt rack and pinion system. It is the only rack railway in Britain, and so it was inevitable that its builders should have turned to Switzerland, where such systems are common, for the technology and equipment. The distinctive nature of the railway's narrow-gauge track, with its parallel toothed racks, can be seen here. The locomotive is equipped with cog wheels that engage with the rack, and these enable it to climb gradients far steeper that would ever be possible with the normal type of adhesion system.

Snowdon Mountain Railway

The rich splendour of Snowdonia's mountain scenery is apparent, even on days of rain and mist. Dwarfed by its surroundings, the diminutive locomotive of the Snowdon Mountain Railway laboriously pushes its single carriage towards the summit, 3,000 feet above sea level. It is a scene that has not changed for a century, and a railway journey without equal in Britain. In the early days of the line, visitors established the pattern of taking the train to the summit, enjoying the views and taking some refreshments, and then walking down, habits that have proved subsequently to be as unchangeable as the railway itself.

Blaenau Ffestiniog

An old crane quietly rusts away at Blaenau Ffestiniog, a rare surviving example of the thousands that were standard equipment in smaller goods yards the length and breadth of Britain. The transportation of local goods was central to the existence of the country railway and, until the 1950s, everything could be sent by train – and it usually was. It was the loss of this vital traffic to the roads that finally brought about the ruination of Britain's rural railway network in the 1960s. This crane was probably used mainly for loading slate on to railway wagons, for it was the slate industry that brought the railways to Blaenau, and considerable prosperity to this remote region in the latter part of the nineteenth century. When the industry died, the railways lingered on, surrounded by decay, a dying town and the mountainous waste tips of the slate quarries. Today, this broken landscape of slate has a remarkable, even picturesque quality, and it is the exciting climax of a scenic and wonderful journey up the Conwy valley from Llandudno.

Blaenau Ffestiniog

Two main lines came to Blaenau Ffestiniog, built by those bitter railway rivals, the GWR and the L&NWR, fighting each other for a share of the slate trade. The L&NWR backed the Conway & Llanrwst Railway, whose line southwards, running along the Conwy valley from Llandudno then through the mountains via Betws-y-Coed and the Lledr valley, was started in 1860 but not completed until 1879. Years of delay were caused by the long tunnel just to the north of Blaenau.

The GWR attacked from the south, in the guise of the Bala & Ffestiniog Railway, and its tortuous, heavily engineered and expensive route eventually reached Blaenau in 1883, by which time the great days of the slate industry were over. The two lines remained firmly apart, with separate stations, until 1961, when the old GWR route was closed down. The Conwy valley line still survives, its approach to Blaenau marked by the distinctive landscape of the slate industry.

Llangollen Railway

A famous railway view is Llangollen station, whose curving platforms stand right beside the fast-flowing waters of the river Dee. The bridge from which this picture was taken carries the main road into the town, whose fine hotels and decorative buildings form an attractive waterfront across the river. Virtually unchanged since the nineteenth century, when the Vale of Llangollen Railway built its line to the town from Ruabon, this view disappeared in 1968 when the railway was closed. Luckily, the station and much of its equipment survived to be subsequently brought back to life as the eastern terminus of the preserved Llangollen Railway. Llangollen now represents a country town station in all its glory, complete with flower beds and a signal box. It was, of course, firmly in GWR territory, but here an elderly LMS tank engine comes to a gentle halt.

Llangollen Railway

In this evocative view, which could have been taken at almost any time since the line opened in 1865, an old steam locomotive hauls its train slowly towards Berwyn's timber-framed station through the woods and hills of the Dee valley, while sheep graze undisturbed. Built originally by the Llangollen & Corwen Railway, the line was part of the GWR's grand plan to open a route across north Wales from its Chester base. Never particularly busy, the line was finally closed in 1968. Since that time, the preserved Llangollen Railway has reopened it in stages, and plans to run trains once again to Corwen by the end of the century. It is a lovely journey, through the green and luxurious valley of the Dee.

Shrewsbury
to Aberystwyth

Shrewsbury's exciting and idiosyncratic Gothic revival station is the starting point for a number of the best railway journeys in Wales, one of which is the line across the country to Aberystwyth. Like so many others, this was constructed in a piecemeal fashion between 1859 and 1863 by a number of small, local companies. These included the Llanidloes & Newtown, the Oswestry & Newtown, the Shrewsbury & Welshpool and the Newtown & Machynlleth, all of which merged in 1864 to form Cambrian Railways. The route, initially following the river Severn across a gently rolling landscape and through old market towns, becomes far more arduous after Newtown. At Talerddig a deep, rock-walled cutting, for years the deepest in the world, was carved through the hills, and from here the line winds its way westwards through wooded hills. This typical view of a green and unpopulated landscape is near Llanbrynmair.

Shrewsbury
to Aberystwyth

The generally restful pace of a country journey allows ample time for the enjoyment of the minutiae of the landscape and the details of railway structures and equipment. The small, independent and largely local companies that created so much of the British network took pride in their buildings, and they were often prepared to spend their money in ways that both respected vernacular traditions and ensured a degree of individuality. All these small companies were quickly absorbed by larger and more ambitious rivals, a pattern that came to its natural conclusion with the establishment, in 1948, of a publicly owned national network. Despite this, much essentially local detail survived, and still gives pleasure today. Machynlleth station, built in 1863 from local stone, still has its decorative barge-boards and ridge tiles in place.

Shrewsbury to Aberystwyth

Many of Britain's country railways are inevitable loss-makers, and probably have never been otherwise. In the past, railway accounting took into consideration social and other non-financial values, and tolerated the support of unprofitable lines by the more profitable routes. In the harsh world of modern economics, this responsible and practical approach is no longer tolerated, and so all these lines face an uncertain future. Many are operated virtually as light railways and minimum maintenance rules apply. As a result, weeds now grow between the tracks and the hedges are not trimmed so often, allowing the railway to become even more a part of its landscape. Here, looking almost like a country lane, the railway from Shrewsbury to the Welsh coast wanders over the hills near Llanbrynmair.

Talyllyn Railway

Wales is the home of the narrow-gauge railway, and the series of lines now operating there is actively promoted as the Great Little Trains of Wales. One of the best known is the Talyllyn, whose seven-mile route from Tywyn on the coast inland to Nant Gwernol was built in 1866 to serve the slate quarries. In 1950, the railway was taken over by a preservation society, and when it reopened in 1951 it became the first in Britain to be rescued and operated by volunteers. A delightful anachronism, whose appeal is increased by the quality of the country through which it runs, the Talyllyn still uses its original locomotives and rolling stock. The railway's distinctive character is apparent in this picture, as the train crosses a a piece of typically green and luscious landscape near Tywyn.

Ffestiniog Railway

There is much more to a railway than simply running trains up and down the tracks. Even the smallest preserved line has to spend time and money in many ways that are often invisible to the travelling public. Typical are the maintenance of track and equipment and the organization of basic supplies, without which the railway would soon grind to a halt. In this view of the Ffestiniog Railway's harbour station at Porthmadog, a diesel locomotive shunts oil wagons while a member of the station staff operates the points. The traditional levers in use are naturally part of the preserved scene, but they are also practical, being tough, durable, easily maintained and far cheaper to install than their modern electronic equivalent.

Ffestiniog Railway

On a fine summer's day, a Ffestiniog Railway locomotive, painted in War Department livery, prepares to haul its heavy train out of Porthmadog station, across the Cobb and up into the hills towards Blaenau Ffestiniog. The Ffestiniog is the best known of the Great Little Trains of Wales. It has an impressive history dating back to 1832, a long climbing route of spectacular beauty, and some unusual double-ended Fairlie locomotives, but its most important claim to fame is that it is a real railway offering a full, year-round public service with mainline connections at each end. It was built originally to transport slate from the quarries around Blaenau down to the harbour at Porthmadog, and until 1863 it was operated by horses and gravity. Tourism, however, has been its mainstay since the 1920s. After a brief period of closure, it was gradually reopened from 1954 as a preserved line.

Shrewsbury to Swansea

The line from Shrewsbury to Swansea, across the heart of Wales, is the rural railway *par excellence*, a meandering and leisurely journey through a lovely and constantly changing landscape to a series of remote villages and small towns that would otherwise be dependent on the private car. The long, 121-mile route was built in the 1860s by a number of small companies notable for their individual approach to architecture. One of these, the Central Wales Railway, was responsible for Knucklas Viaduct, 13 grand arches whose rough, freestone finish and castellations, complete with arrow slits, were apparently inspired by the nearby ruins of Knucklas Castle. Its remarkable appearance underlines the desire of Victorian railway engineers to create, even on minor lines, memorable structures that contributed to their environment.

Shrewsbury to Swansea

On a warm afternoon at Dolau station, a little flower-bedecked halt in the middle of nowhere, the train pauses on its long journey from Swansea to Shrewsbury and an old man steps out, returning from a visit to Llandrindod Wells. He collects his bicycle from the bushes beside the wooden station hut, where he had left it earlier in the day, waits for the train to depart, and then wheels it along the platform and over the level crossing before riding slowly away into the distance. It is a timeless country railway scene, and one that justifies the continued existence of these rural lines that are still the social and economic mainstay of the remote regions they serve. It also underscores the value of the real, as opposed to the preserved, railway.

The North

'There is a railway line in England which fights its way over the gaunt Pennine uplands to make a vital communication between north and south. A line which tested to the utmost the peerless constructional skill of British railway engineers. A line which braves the rugged contours of wild fell and striding dale, and which defies the freakish, unpredictable weather of its chosen path.' This is a fitting description of the Settle to Carlisle line, the most spectacular railway journey in England, and one whose current popularity is the result of the long battle in the early 1990s to save it from closure. At the heart of this battle was the need to maintain the great Ribblehead, or Batty Moss viaduct, whose 24 arches carry the line for 440 yards up to 165 feet above the inhospitable terrain.

The north of England is rightly considered to be the birthplace of the railway. Miles of horse-drawn tramways were built in the eighteenth century to carry coal from the mines to the ports for onward shipment, and some of the first steam locomotives were in use early in the nineteenth century. It was against this background that the Stockton & Darlington, the world's first passenger-carrying steam railway, was opened in 1825. George and Robert Stephenson, Britain's pioneering railway engineers, came from the north east but their impact was felt all across the country. Coal, iron, industry and the needs of passengers were the inspiration that built the first lines from London to Liverpool, Manchester and Leeds, all open by 1840, and the first coast-to-coast railway between Newcastle and Carlisle, completed two years earlier. From this point, the railways spread at an astonishing rate. The first trans-Pennine route, linking Leeds and Manchester, was opened in 1841, and others rapidly followed. Indeed, rivalry between railway companies ensured that new routes across the Pennines continued to be built throughout the nineteenth century, with the last one being completed in the 1890s. Elsewhere, lines were built along the east and west coasts, sometimes as part of routes to Scotland, and sometimes to satisfy the needs of local industry and, increasingly, tourism in the latter part of the century. It was tourism, for example, that inspired the building of the railways to the Lake District and along the coastline of North Yorkshire.

Landscape is the dominant feature in the north, and it determined the character of the railways of the region. The way the railway builders responded to the challenge of that landscape can be seen in the legacy of great engineering features, the massive viaducts, long tunnels and towering embankments they created to enable their trains to cross the rugged and inhospitable terrain. These great structures also underline the way the railway contributed to the landscape, and matched its natural grandeur in both scale and detail.

Settle to Carlisle

The building of the Settle to Carlisle line was inspired by the ambitions of the Midland Railway, which wanted its own route to Scotland, in direct competition with the west and east coast main lines operated by the London & North Western and the Great Northern companies. The building of the line, across 72 miles of the most remote and exposed landscape in England, was the greatest achievement of the Midland's chief engineer, J S Crossley. It was completed in 1875, having cost £3.5 million, and probably never justified, or recovered, either this huge expenditure or the Herculean efforts involved in its creation. Fifteen tunnels were necessary, and the greatest of these is Blea Moor, which is 1 mile 869 yards long and up to 500 feet deep through Pennine rocks. Here, the line curves away from the tunnel's northern mouth into a typical Pennine landscape, which is daunting even on a fine summer's day.

There were, of course, country railways in the north, lines built to serve old market towns and quiet agricultural regions, and branches wandering up remote river valleys. Most of these have now gone, and the great country railways of the north today are those lines that survive despite the odds, lines that are fragments of former networks, and lines that live on regardless, even though the forces that brought them to life – industry or tourism – have faded away. Any list of the best railway journeys in Britain would have to include the former Midland Railway trans-Pennine route from Settle to Carlisle and the old Cumbrian coastline from Carlisle to Lancaster, railways that even in their quiet retirement still carry the clear stamp of history. The country railways of the north are peopled with the ghosts of the great engineers, and of those Victorian entrepreneurs who worked so hard to develop their land into the engine room of Britain's nineteenth-century prosperity, but they are friendly ghosts that add to the pleasures of the journey. Even the preserved lines have a rugged and exciting individuality that ensure they play their part in keeping alive the pageant of history.

Settle to Carlisle

Most of the stations between Settle and Carlisle are, by definition, remote and rugged. Built of local materials, they are in a style created for the line by Crossley and reflect the vernacular traditions of the region. Typical is Dent, with its gables, barge-boarding and tall chimneys, and there can be no more gloriously placed station in England. In the summer, this station is a favourite with walkers, but for much of the year it is a bleak and inaccessible place.

Settle to Carlisle

As this sign, in the old LMS colours, states Dent is, at 1150 feet above sea level, the highest mainline station in England. It is not the highest point on the line between Settle and Carlisle, however. This honour goes to Ais Gill summit, 1,169 feet above sea level. The highest mainline summit in Britain, 1,484 feet above sea level, is at Druimuachdar, on the line between Perth and Inverness. The challenging terrain of the north of Britain posed problems to all the engineers building lines in the region, and each one had a preferred solution. Some favoured tunnels and viaducts, which were expensive and difficult to build and maintain, but which allowed for a more level route. Others, often those with smaller budgets, were forced to use the steep gradients that are a feature of the West Coast main line at Shap and the former Caledonian line at Beattock, gradients that were punishing to both locomotives and their crews.

Settle to Carlisle

A ruined or disused gangers' hut is a familiar track-side sight all over Britain, and a lasting record of the way the railways were maintained in the old days. Small and sometimes elegant little buildings, made from brick, stone or the characteristic concrete of the Southern Railway, and always marked by a strong chimney, these huts offered shelter and a secure store for tools and equipment to generations of men whose job it was to patrol and maintain the track,s year in and year out. This tumbledown example is near Dent Head viaduct, on the Settle to Carlisle line. In the bleak Pennine winter, the shelter offered by the hut and the warmth of its fire represented the difference between life and death for the men working to maintain track and equipment in the most inhospitable of conditions. Today, this type of lineside hut has largely been rendered obsolete.

Middlesborough to Whitby

Disused station buildings quietly decaying and an overgrown platform are romantic but sad relics of a once great railway network, and an all too familiar feature of Britain's rural lines. This station is on the Esk valley line, a beautiful but little used route between Middlesborough and Whitby. Today, it is just a long and leisurely branch line barely clinging to life, but in the past it was the backbone of an extensive local network, the construction of which was inspired both by freight and by the development of tourism along the north Yorkshire coast. Much of it was built by George Hudson, the great entrepreneur and visionary and Britain's first railway millionaire. By 1846, he controlled nearly half of Britain's railways, but ten years later he was bankrupt. The distinctive style of the stone-built Esk valley stations can be seen here.

Middlesborough to Whitby

The line to Whitby from Middlesborough sweeps across Kildale Moor, a typical north Yorkshire landscape near Commondale. This section was built from 1846 by George Hudson's York & North Midland Railway, along with an expanding network of lines that linked the communities of Stockton, Darlington, Middlesborough, Guisborough and Northallerton. Later, when the whole network had become a part of the North Eastern Railway, other lines were built northwards from Whitby along the coast via Saltburn and Redcar, and southwards to Scarborough. All this disappeared in the late 1950s and the 1960s, and even the Whitby line was scheduled for closure, but it was reprieved at the last moment. Today, it lingers on, a delightful exploration of the landscape as well as a lifeline for the moorland villages along the route.

Middlesborough to Whitby

Just outside of Whitby, the sweeping curves of the river Esk are spanned by the 13 great brick arches of the Larpool viaduct. Completed in 1885, it carried the line that ran southwards from Whitby along the coast to Scarborough, a dramatic and steeply graded cliff-top route. Trains on this line ran into Whitby's West Cliff station, high above the town, and then backed down a long, steep curve into the elegant 1847 town station. This line, and the West Cliff station, closed in 1965, but the viaduct still stands, now as important and as striking a feature of the landscape as Whitby's famous abbey. A little train on the surviving Esk valley line to Whitby can be seen passing under the viaduct, having departed from the sad remains of Whitby's once splendid classical terminus, built in 1847 to the designs of G T Andrews, George Hudson's stylish architect.

Middlesborough to Whitby

Much of the route of
the line to Whitby follows
closely the Esk valley, and it
criss crosses the river many
times. Here, near Danby, in
the North Yorkshire Moors
National Park, the Esk is
little more than a stream,
hidden by trees at the
bottom of a wide and gently
sloping valley randomly
patterned by green fields,
hedges and stone walls, and
populated only by solitary
farms. Dropping down
towards its estuary at Whitby,
and never far from the
railway, that stream quickly
becomes a fast-flowing river.
Danby station, with its
traditional rough-stone finish
and stepped gables, is just
to the west of the picture,
and nearby in its village is
a medieval bridge, a ruined
castle, a fine church and
an old mill – a picturesque
group that makes it well
worth getting off the train.

North Yorkshire Moors Railway

The ending of mainline
steam in Britain in 1968
brought with it the closure
of all the locomotive
maintenance workshops. The
major preserved lines have,
therefore, had to establish
their own repair, restoration
and maintenance facilities to
keep elderly locomotives in
tip-top condition. The North
Yorkshire Moors Railway has
created a typically extensive
and well-equipped workshop
complex at its Grosmont
headquarters, capable of
rebuilding and maintaining
large mainline locomotives.
Here, in a stripped down
and unrecognizable form, the
former Southern Railway
West Country class Bulleid
Pacific Taw Valley undergoes
a boiler test following a
complete rebuild.

North Yorkshire Moors Railway

The first railway to reach Whitby was the horse-drawn Whitby & Pickering, whose Esk valley and moorland route via Grosmont was completed in 1836. This became the foundation for the region's expanding network after its purchase by George Hudson's York & North Midland company in 1845, and rapid conversion to steam haulage. The Whitby to Grosmont section remains in use as part of the Esk valley line, but the section south from Grosmont was closed in 1965, and then subsequently reopened by the North Yorkshire Moors Railway, one of the longest and most exciting of Britain's preserved lines. Here, in the magnificent setting of Goathland Moor, one of the railway's steam locomotives hauls its long train towards Grosmont, around the sweeping curves below Northdale Scar.

North Yorkshire Moors Railway

Railway relics are widely collected, and there are certain auction companies that hold regular specialist sales of old signs, station and railway equipment, posters, printed ephemera and bits of old locomotives. Preserved railways are, of course, the major holders of such material, and their stations are often virtual museums of railway relics. The aim is always the re-creation of a distinct period flavour, based on an eye for detail that links together history and fantasy in an enjoyable manner. Everyone remembers, or likes to think they remember, stations lit by gas or oil lamps, and so this traditional oil lamp at Goathland station on the North Yorkshire Moors Railway gives the right atmosphere. The platform indicator shows that a southbound train is due.

Ravenglass & Eskdale Railway

Against a spectacular backdrop of Cumbrian hills, a crowded train on the Ravenglass & Eskdale Railway meanders along its little 15-inch-gauge track near Muncaster Mill. This seven-mile line, one of Britain's most popular and most scenic narrow-gauge railways, has had a chequered history. It was built in the early 1870s to carry haematite from quarries in the hills near Boot to the coast at Ravenglass. Passenger carrying started in 1876. Continuous financial problems plagued it until its closure in 1908. Rebuilt to a 15-inch gauge, it reopened after the First World War, largely to cater to the developing tourist market. It struggled on until 1958, when it was, once again, put up for sale. Bought by a preservation society, it has since become a great success, and operates as a proper public railway, with all-year service and a mainline connection at Ravenglass.

Ravenglass & Eskdale Railway

In the sheds at Ravenglass, one of the railway's small-scale but impressive locomotives is prepared for the hard day's work ahead. Independent and self-reliant, the Ratty – as the Ravenglass & Eskdale Railway is popularly known – builds and maintains its own locomotives and rolling stock. Despite its size, it is a real railway. It has a long history and it offers its visitors a very complete railway experience, along with some splendid scenery. It is much used by walkers, and there are even some old camping coaches for visitors who want to spend time exploring the railway and its setting. The railway has also restored the old water mill at Muncaster, and this now grinds the flour sold in the souvenir shops.

Cumbrian coast

Railways came early to
Cumbria, inspired by the
huge local deposits of coal,
iron ore and, ultimately,
haematite, and by 1850 a line
was open all along the coast
from Carlisle southwards
towards Lancaster. A number
of companies were involved
it its creation – such as the
Maryport & Carlisle, the
Whitehaven Junction and
the Ulverstone & Lancaster –
and from it an extensive
network spread into the hilly
hinterlands. The impact of
the railway turned Maryport,
Workington, Whitehaven and
Barrow into flourishing ports
and centres of industry, and
then tourism brought the
railways even greater success.
Today, the mines are closed,
industry has largely gone,
tourism has faded away and
all that remains is the
original Cumbrian coast
line, offering its occasional
passengers more miles of
seaside than any other rail
journey in Britain.

Cumbrian coast

This page shows a view of
the quieter coastal landscape
to be found south of
Ravenglass, but more
dramatic is the route of the
Cumbrian line southwards
from Workington and
Whitehaven. For miles, the
train runs virtually on the
beach as the line follows the
twists and turns of the rocky
shore. In winter, the train is
often hidden by the clouds
of salty spray thrown up by
the crashing waves, and in
summer the journey is a rich
exploration of extravagant
colours and dramatic skies.
The route is a romantic
one through an empty and
exciting landscape, marked
by the overgrown traces
of industry, quietly dying
villages and the sad ghosts of
once-ambitious tourism. It is
a little used but socially vital
line, ironically kept open
by the needs of the nuclear
power plant installation at
Sellafield, a few miles to the
south of this typical coastal
view near Braystones.

Cumbrian coast

Ulverston station is notable, above all else, for its fine ironwork, the richly decorative detailing of which underlines the excellence that was a characteristic of the Furness Railway. In the latter half of the nineteenth century, it was one of the most prosperous railways in Britain, thanks to its exploitation of the vast haematite deposits north of Barrow. It built and owned hundreds of miles of lines, it established the town of Barrow with its extensive docks and, when industry began to fade, it pioneered the development of tourism in the region, creating many Morecambe Bay and Lakeland resorts. With its elegant, red-liveried trains, its concern for fine architecture, and its pretty cast-iron station seats that featured a squirrel support, the Furness remained one of Britain's most stylish independent railways until 1923.

Cumbrian coast

With its delicate platform canopies and grand Italianate clock tower, Ulverston station is a splendid sight, and a rare survival at a time when accountants have little patience with such expensive and antique frivolities. The best building in the town, and Ulverston's third station on this site, it was created in 1873 by Paley & Austin for the Furness Railway in a manner that adequately reflected that company's ambitious development of tourism in the region. Today, few trains visit the platforms that once thronged with well-dressed and elegant visitors, drawn by the delights of Windermere and the lakes, and the sands of Morecambe Bay, all of which are easily accessible from Ulverston via the Furness Railway.

Cumbrian coast

Weeds on the platform and
some battered old hand-
lettered steps highlight the
precarious nature of Britain's
country railways in the
current climate of minimum
maintenance and inadequate
public funding. These steps,
which are by no means
unusual, are made necessary
by the design of modern
trains, whose door sills are
now higher than many of the
old stations they serve. These
steps are to be found at
Silecroft on the Cumbrian
coastline north of Millom.
In time, they will also
become part of the history
of the rural railway, and be
displayed in some museum
as a curious relic.

Cumbrian coast

Sweeping along the northern
shore of Morecambe Bay,
past stations with such
emotive names as Cark &
Cartmell and Grange-over-
Sands, the Cumbrian coastline
then crosses the sandy
estuary of the river Kent
on a long, low viaduct. At
its southern end is Arnside,
whose painted houses can
just be seen above the trees.
From here, an old line, long
closed, ran up beside the
Kent towards Oxenholme,
passing the vast expanse
of Milnthorpe Sands to
the north of the viaduct.
A journey along the
Cumbrian coastline is a
succession of rich panoramas,
with the constantly changing
seaside on one side and, on
the other, the distant views
of Lakeland hills, full of
gloriously subtle colours
in the evening light.

Scotland

Railways in Scotland have a long and remarkable history. One of the first lines, the Kilmarnock & Troon, opened in 1812, was built to carry coal. It went on, however, to be the first to use a steam locomotive, in 1817, and the first to carry passengers. Much of the country's network had been completed by the 1850s, inspired largely by the needs of industry and the coal mines, and two of its largest railways, the North British and the Caledonian, date from 1838 and 1845 respectively. This pattern of development continued through the nineteenth century, despite the rugged landscape and the relatively small size of the population. Much of the network was, inevitably, in the Lowlands and centred around Glasgow, Edinburgh and the major industrial centres, but there were many lines radiating outwards from Scotland's economic and social heartlands to serve country regions, the developing tourist areas and, ultimately, the Highlands. From Inverness, the home of the Highland Railway, lines radiated outwards to serve the needs of Britain's most northerly regions. Among the last to be completed were the lines from Fort William to Mallaig, and Inverness to Kyle of Lochalsh, lines that reflect better than almost any in Britain the railway's dramatic response to the challenge posed by a demanding landscape.

Despite its social importance in a country whose rural regions were dependent on the railway, the Scottish network was severely pruned during the 1960s and 1970s. As usual, the country lines were particularly hard hit, and large areas – for example, Kirkcudbright and the north of Aberdeen – suddenly found themselves without any railways at all. Surprisingly, the Highland lines were not drastically cut. Some secondary and branch lines were lost, along with much of the local network around Perth and Dundee, but there were some remarkable survivals, including the lines to Oban, Mallaig, Kyle of Lochalsh and Wick and Thurso. The continued existence of these and other similar lines means that Scotland, like Wales, is today one of the last bastions of the real country

Crianlarich to Oban

The line curves around the head of Loch Awe, passing the ruins of Kilchurn Castle, the Campbell stronghold, and then the train pauses at Loch Awe station. Recently reopened after a period of closure, the station has its own pier for steamer trips on the loch and, more important, a restaurant in the form of an old carriage parked on a siding. A grand Victorian mansion in baronial style stands above the station, a fitting reflection of the extensive development of the Highlands in the late nineteenth century that was inspired by the railways. Considering the wild nature and relative emptiness of the landscape, and the small number of train users outside of the holiday season, it is remarkable that railways still survive in the Highlands.

railway. Travellers can still enjoy a great variety of long and leisurely journeys through the most remote and inaccessible regions, surrounded all the time by the most spectacular scenery and, on a good day, by the most glorious colours. The train to Kyle of Lochalsh, or even more so to Wick and Thurso, is simply one of the best railway experiences in Britain and, probably, mainland Europe as well. The special qualities of the Scottish landscape would seem to make such lines now entirely dependent upon the whims of tourism. While that is important, it is not enough, for the long term survival of these routes is vital for Scotland to have any hope of maintaining a viable public transport network into the future.

Despite the obvious appeal of the landscape and its tourist potential, there are few preserved lines in Scotland. None of the attractive routes lost during the closures have since been reopened. The few that do exist are more interesting as railway museums than as country railways. It may well be that with so many splendid routes still in operation, the preserved railway has little to offer.

Fort William to Mallaig

Inspired by the battle between two railway giants, the Caledonian and the North British, for the west coast fish trade, the West Highland Railway was incorporated in 1889. Its route from Glasgow, initially along the Clyde and Loch Lomond, and then high across the wilds of Rannoch Moor, was slow and expensive to build, and it did not reach Fort William until 1894. The final section, a spectacular journey and one of the best in Britain, from Fort William to the sea at Mallaig, was not finished until 1901. The route, initially along the shore of Loch Eil and then across the mountains, includes many rock cuttings, 11 tunnels and steep gradients. Here, on its way towards Glenfinnan, the line carves its way through a remote and rocky valley.

Fort William to Mallaig

The Fort William to Mallaig line is marked by its dramatic engineering and there are a number of viaducts along the route. Justly the most famous is at Glenfinnan, whose 21 curving arches have featured in innumerable postcard, book and calendar views. more than 400 yards long, this delicate structure is built from concrete, at the time of its construction a pioneering use of a new material on so large a scale. The viaduct stands at the head of Loch Shiel, whose waters can be seen in the distance in this view towards the south. This also underlines the great appeal of any Highland journey – the constantly changing patterns of light and colour in the landscape.

Fort William to Mallaig

Dwarfed by the distant peaks of Meall'na h Airigh, Meall a Bhainne and Sgorr nan Cearc, the line to Mallaig crosses a valley near Glenfinnan, bathed in summer colours. This is the best known of the Highland journeys, its popularity having been increased in recent years by the regular use of steam specials during the summer season and by a number of tourist trains. With all freight a distant memory, including the once crucial fish traffic, it is only tourism that keeps these real country railways open.

Fort William to Mallaig

Near Lochailort station a remote Catholic church, now sadly redundant, stands on a headland above Loch Ailort. The railway runs past the head of the loch, crossing over the river Eilt, and then cuts its way through the rocky landscape to its first view of the Atlantic, far above the wild and inaccessible bays of Loch nan Uamh. For years the railway brought life and hope to this remote region of Scotland, but those days are gone, leaving the line's future dependent on the uncertain whims of the tourist industry.

Kyle of Lochalsh to Inverness

In 1865, the Highland Railway was formed, with Inverness as the hub of its small but rugged empire. Lines ran to the west, the east and the south, but particularly important was the route westwards along the Beauly Firth and up to Dingwall, the starting point for great journeys to the far north and the Atlantic coast. After leaving Inverness, the train comes quickly to the river Ness and Telford's famous Caledonian Canal at Clachnaharry. A delightful anachronism, an old 1909 swing bridge carries the line across the canal, still controlled by a traditional signal box. The bridge is still regularly opened to allow the passage of fishing boats and pleasure craft using this major waterway, which crosses the country from Inverness to Fort William via Loch Ness. Such links with the past are a feature of Highland journeys.

Kyle of Lochalsh to Inverness

In the lovely colours of a truly glorious summer's day, the line from Inverness to Kyle of Lochalsh skirts the head of Loch Luichart. Nearby are the buildings of Britain's first hydroelectric scheme, opened in 1954. Much of the line to Kyle was built by the Dingwall & Skye Railway, a small company that, despite huge costs and formidable engineering, managed to reach Strome Ferry, at the mouth of Loch Carron, in 1870. The company then ran out of money and despite merging with the Highland Railway no further progress was made. Thus, Strome Ferry was to remain the line's western terminus for the next 27 years.

Kyle of Lochalsh to Inverness

With a remote route that winds its way around lochs and across tumbling rivers, the Kyle line explores some of the best railway scenery in Britain. The stations are often minimal structures serving small, isolated communities that for years were totally dependent on the railway. Typical is Achanalt, a few houses clustered around the little station in the distance in this view. It is difficult today to grasp the complete inaccessibility of such communities prior to the coming of the railway.

Kyle of Lochalsh to Inverness

From Achanalt to Achnasheen the railway follows the river Bran across an empty landscape of heath and moorland broken by small lochs, and with ever-changing views of distant mountains. In the golden light of a late summer's day, the line cuts straight across the landscape beside the meandering river and, in the distance, is the purple peak of Sgurr a'Ghlas Leathaid. The pleasures to be had from such a journey are limitless, at almost any time of year, and they underline the importance of Scotland as one of the last homes of the real country railway.

Kyle of Lochalsh to Inverness

From Strathcarron to Strome Ferry, the railway line runs for miles along the southern shore of Loch Carron, and this sunset view of the line curving along the lochside near Attadale shows the particular quality of light that is so very characteristic of the region. From the train can be seen a series of wonderful panoramas across the loch, while ahead is the distant shape of Skye, closing the horizon.

Kyle of Lochalsh to Inverness

Three new stations were built between Strome Ferry and Kyle of Lochalsh, Duncraig, Plockton and Duirinish – with Plockton the only one serving a community of any size. All are little used now, but some distinctive features survive, notably the famous octagonal waiting room at Duncraig, a typically eccentric and characterful piece of railway architecture. West of Duncraig, the line offers a fine view of Plockton's pretty harbour.

Kyle of Lochalsh to Inverness

Set on the water's edge below steeply wooded hills, Strome Ferry was for years the western terminus of the line from Inverness. In 1893, the Highland Railway decided to complete the line to Kyle of Lochalsh, but it took four years to build the the ten miles that remained. Most of the route for the railway had to be carved along the steep lochside out of solid rock, and it required 31 cuttings and 29 bridges. The final cost was more than £20,000 per mile and, at the time, it was the most expensive stretch of railway ever built. The completion of the line opened up a direct route to the Isles, and the railway was soon busy with both freight and passenger traffic. The legacy of all that money and hard work is a splendid, but little used, scenic journey.

Kyle of Lochalsh to Inverness

Kyle of Lochalsh station really is the end of the line and the rails and the platform finish virtually at the water's edge. It is a magnificent site, carved out of solid rock, and surrounded by colourful cottages and fishing boats. Just across the water are the purple hills of Skye, an incomparable setting for Britain's best-placed railway terminus. In this view, a warship moored at the deep-water quay forms an unusual backdrop for the train waiting to depart for Inverness. In the past a busy station for both freight and passengers, Kyle is now little used and faces a difficult future, one probably made even more uncertain by the new road bridge to Skye.

Inverness to Thurso

Many of the stations of the line from Inverness to Wick and Thurso are stone-built, single-storey structures in a local croft style, designed by their Victorian architects to blend in with the landscape. Typical is Forsinard, a remote station in the wilds of Caithness. In this view, taken on a wet and grey day that has given a gloss to the old wooden platform, the station with its signal box and screen of trees looks quite domestic, even suburban. This is misleading, however, for people leaving a train here and walking away from the station will quickly find themselves in the middle of nowhere, with only the wild moorland and the river Halladale for company.

Inverness to Thurso

The most exciting and extraordinary railway journey in Britain is the line northwards from Inverness to Wick and Thurso, more than 160 miles of meandering travel across a wild and inaccessible landscape. That such a line was ever built is remarkable, and that it survives today is even more so. Completed in 1874, the line was constructed in stages by the Highland Railway, the Sutherland Railway and the Sutherland & Caithness Railway. A major backer was the Duke of Sutherland, who not only contributed thousands, but also built and operated, at his own expense, the important coastal section between Golspie and Helmsdale. A relic of those days is the Duke's private station at Dunrobin, a pretty, timber-framed structure. Above all else a line for landscape, the railway explores the coastline, the hills, the rivers and the huge tracts of remote moorland, as in this view near Altnabreac.

Inverness to Thurso

In the flat moorland landscape, which stretches for miles without interruption beneath huge skies, the train stands out on the horizon. In the foreground is Loch Caise, near Altnabreac, one of the most remote and inaccessible stations in Britain. In this area, deer are more common than people, particularly since the notorious clearances of the nineteenth century, and wandering herds can often be seen from the train. The journey to Wick or Thurso is a great adventure, and quite unlike anything else in Britain. The indirect route from Inverness, at times along the coast, and at times sweeping inland into the wildest regions, takes several hours to reach the very top of Britain where, in summer, the short nights are broken by the continuous screaming of the gulls.

Inverness to Thurso

Scotscalder station, and others like it at Altnabreac and Kildonan, stand absolutely in the middle of nowhere. Built originally to serve hunting lodges, they cling on to life in the most precarious manner. Trains still stop and, occasionally, people get off and disappear into the empty wilderness. At other times, however, the passing train is the only sign of life as it crosses a landscape of brilliant summer colour beneath a huge and dramatic sky. In the distance, Ben Dorrery squats on the horizon.

Strathspey Railway

Despite the massive closures of the 1960s that decimated the Scottish railway network, and particularly its rural routes, there are few preserved railways north of the border. One of the best known is the Strathspey Railway, which has brought back to life a short stretch of the former Highland Railway Aviemore to Forres line, which was originally part of the old main line from Perth to Inverness. Traditionally dressed in faded overalls and greasetop hat, a Strathspey driver awaits his tour of duty in his immaculate cab.

Strathspey Railway

Surrounded by steam and beneath clouds of dense black smoke, an old industrial saddle tank locomotive, now enjoying a new lease of life on the preserved Strathspey Railway, hauls its train slowly out of Boat of Garten station. The railway operates its trains between Boat of Garten and Aviemore, adjacent to the station on the Perth to Inverness main line. Boat of Garten is a classic Highland Railway station, with typical iron latticework footbridge. The distinctive flavour of Scotland's railway past comes to life here, preserving the spirit of a country that was, in its heyday, the real home of Britain's rural railways.

Railways to visit

This list includes details of the country railways and the preserved lines in this book. Inevitably, these represent only a selection of those operating throughout Britain. For information about other country railways, consult local and national timetables and railway information offices. For information about other preserved lines, consult tourist information centres, railway magazines and other specialist publications, or the Association of Railway Preservation Societies.

It is not possible to give the operating companies of all the present British Rail country lines, since these are all in the privatization melting pot, and will not be resolved by the time of this book's publication.

WEST COUNTRY

Country Railways

St Erth to St Ives
Short branch line from the main Exeter to Penzance railway

Plymouth to Gunnislake
Long branch line from Plymouth

Liskeard to Looe
Short branch line from the main Exeter to Penzance railway

Exeter to Barnstaple
Long branch line from Exeter

Other country railways in Cornwall and Devon

Truro to Falmouth branch line

Par to Newquay branch line

Exeter to Exmouth branch line

Preserved Lines

Bodmin & Wenford Railway
Bodmin General Station
Bodmin
Cornwall PL31 1AQ
Tel: 01208 73666

Paignton & Dartmouth Railway
Queens Park Station
Paignton
Devon TQ4 6AF
Tel: 01803 555872

THE SOUTH

Country Railways

Weymouth to Bath and Bristol
Long cross-country secondary line

Hastings to Ashford
Long cross-country and coastal secondary line

Other country railways in the South

Reading to Tonbridge line

Maidenhead to Marlow branch line

Twyford to Henley branch line

Preserved Lines

Isle of Wight Steam Railway
Haven Street Station
Ryde
Isle of Wight PO33 4DS
Tel: 01983 882204

Mid-Hants Railway
Alresford Station
Alresford
Hampshire SO24 9JG
Tel: 0196273 3810

Romney, Hythe & Dymchurch Railway
New Romney Station
Kent
Tel: 01679 62353

Swanage Railway
The Station
Swanage
Dorset BH19 1HB
Tel: 01929 425800

EAST ANGLIA

Country Railways

Marks Tey (Colchester) to Sudbury
Short branch from main London to East Anglia line

Ipswich to Lowestoft
Cross-country secondary line from Ipswich

Norwich to Sheringham
Long branch line from Norwich

Other country railways in East Anglia

Norwich to Yarmouth (two routes)

Norwich to Lowestoft

Norwich to Cambridge

Preserved Lines

North Norfolk Railway
The Station
Sheringham
Norfolk NR26 8RA
Tel: 01263 822045

Wells & Walsingham Railway
Stiffkey Road
Wells-next-the-Sea
Norfolk

THE MIDLANDS

Country Railways

Bedford to Bletchley
Cross-country secondary line

Derby to Matlock
Long branch line

Manchester to Buxton
Long branch line

Shrewsbury to Newport
Cross-country secondary route

Other country railways in the Midlands

Ely to Leicester

Stoke-on-Trent to Derby

Oxford to Hereford

Preserved Lines

Great Central Railway
Loughborough Central Station
Great Central Road
Loughborough
Leicestershire LE11 1SS
Tel: 01509 230726

Severn Valley Railway
The Railway Station
Bewdley
Worcestershire DT12 1BG
Tel: 01299 403816

WALES

Country Railways

Llandudno Junction to Blaenau
Ffestiniog
Long branch line

Shrewsbury to Aberystwyth
Long cross-country secondary line

Shrewsbury to Pwllheli
Long cross-country and coastal
secondary line

Shrewsbury to Swansea
Long cross-country secondary line

Other country railways in Wales

Carmarthen to Pembroke

Valley lines from Cardiff and Swansea

Shrewsbury to Chester

Preserved Lines

Ffestiniog Railway
Harbour Station
Porthmadog
Gwynedd LL49 9NF
Tel: 01766 512340

Llangollen Railway
Llangollen Station
Abbey Road
Llangollen
Clwyd LL20 8SN
Tel: 01978 860951

Snowdon Mountain Railway
Llanberis
nr Caernarfon
Gwynedd LL55 4TY
Tel: 01286 870223

Talyllyn Railway
Wharfe Station
Tywyn
Gwynedd LL36 9EY
Tel: 01654 710472

THE NORTH

Country Railways

Carlisle to Lancaster
Long coastal secondary route

Middlesborough to Whitby
Long cross-country branch line

Settle to Carlisle
Long cross-country secondary line

Other country railways in the North

Carlisle to Newcastle

York to Scarborough

Preserved Lines

North Yorkshire Moors Railway
Pickering Station
Pickering
North Yorkshire
Tel: 01751 72508

Ravenglass & Eskdale Railway
Ravenglass
Cumbria CA18 1SW
Tel: 01229 717171

SCOTLAND

Country Railways

Crianlarich to Oban
Long cross-country branch line

Fort William to Mallaig
Long cross-country branch line

Inverness to Kyle of Lochalsh
Long cross-country branch line

Inverness to Wick and Thurso
Long cross-country branch line

Other country railways in Scotland

Ayr to Stranraer

Glasgow to Fort William

Inverness to Aberdeen

Perth to Inverness

Preserved Line

Strathspey Railway
The Station
Boat of Garten
Inverness-shire PH24 3BH
Tel: 0147983 692

Index